T0274587

"We live in serious times w   nd
a growing secularism rise: is-
tianity. God raises up strc   , so
thanks be to God, my close friend of many years has written
The Jesus Book to turn back the tide of biblical illiteracy
and inspirationally equip every pastor and Christian to hold
up the standard of the Bible as our only hope in a truth-
confused world."

Dr. David Jeremiah,
author, founder, and host of *Turning Point for God*,
senior pastor of Shadow Mountain Community Church

"Many modern theologians attempt to separate Jesus from
His Word, presenting Him as merely a tolerant teacher, powerless and perfectly palatable for our progressive age. But it is
only through Scripture that we meet the real Jesus—the Creator of the universe, the Alpha and Omega, our Defender,
our Righteousness, and our only Salvation. Dr. Graham
brilliantly explains how, from beginning to end, the Bible
is "the Jesus Book"—a Book worth trusting, studying, and
understanding."

Allie Beth Stuckey,
host of the podcast *Relatable*

"If you're interested in knowing the Bible more but struggle to make it part of your daily life, don't miss Dr. Jack
Graham's new book, *The Jesus Book: Reading and Understanding the Bible for Yourself*. This book offers clear guidance, practical insight, and simple tools to help you find
hope, reassurance, and purpose through God's Word. It is a
must-read for anyone seeking to deepen their faith in God."

Craig Groeschel,
pastor of Life.Church,
New York Times bestselling author

"*The Jesus Book* is a powerful guide to understanding the Bible on your own. With profound insights and practical wisdom, Jack Graham empowers you to discover God's Word like never before. This is a must-read for anyone eager to deepen their understanding of Scripture and grow in their faith!"

Greg Laurie,
senior pastor of Harvest Christian Fellowship

The
JESUS
BOOK

Books by Jack Graham

From Bethany House Publishers

Unseen:
Angels, Satan, Heaven, Hell, and Winning the Battle for Eternity

Angels:
Who They Are, What They Do, and Why It Matters

Reignite:
Fresh Focus for an Enduring Faith

The Jesus Book:
Reading and Understanding the Bible for Yourself

The
JESUS
BOOK

READING AND UNDERSTANDING
THE BIBLE FOR YOURSELF

JACK GRAHAM

BETHANYHOUSE
a division of Baker Publishing Group
Minneapolis, Minnesota

© 2024 by Jack Graham

Published by Bethany House Publishers
Minneapolis, Minnesota
BethanyHouse.com

Bethany House Publishers is a division of
Baker Publishing Group, Grand Rapids, Michigan

Printed in the United States of America

Library of Congress Cataloging-in-Publication Data

Names: Graham, Jack, author.
Title: The Jesus book : reading and understanding the Bible for yourself / Jack Graham.
Description: Minneapolis, Minnesota : Bethany House Publishers, a division of Baker Publishing Group, [2024] | Includes bibliographical references.
Identifiers: LCCN 2024008555 | ISBN 9780764243776 (paper) | ISBN 9780764243912 (casebound) | ISBN 9781493448012 (ebook)
Subjects: LCSH: Bible—Devotional use. | Bible—Reading.
Classification: LCC BS617.G59 2024 | DDC 242/.5—dc23/eng/20240515
LC record available at https://lccn.loc.gov/2024008555

Cover design by Peter Gloege, Look Design Studio

Baker Publishing Group publications use paper produced from sustainable forestry practices and postconsumer waste whenever possible.

24   25   26   27   28   29   30   7   6   5   4   3   2   1

To the people of Prestonwood Baptist Church, whose love for God's Word and commitment to the proclamation of Christ to the ends of the earth have inspired me every day since becoming pastor in 1989. With extreme gratitude for your faithfulness to love, honor, and serve Jesus till the whole world hears.

> *Now to him who is able to do far more abundantly than all that we ask or think, according to the power at work within us, to him be glory in the church and in Christ Jesus throughout all generations, forever and ever. Amen.*
>
> *Ephesians 3:20–21*

So the word of God became a human being and lived among us.

We saw his splendour (the splendour as of a father's only son), full of grace and truth.

John 1:14 PHILLIPS

CONTENTS

INTRODUCTION

We must allow the Word of God to confront us, to
disturb our security, to undermine our complacency,
and to overthrow our patterns of thought and behavior.

John Stott

I can't remember a time in my life when the Bible was
not with me. In many ways I can relate to Timothy in the
New Testament, whom the apostle Paul described by saying "from infancy you have known the Holy Scriptures"
(2 Timothy 3:15 NIV). As a small boy, I was often in my
maternal grandfather's lap, listening as he read the Bible
out loud to me almost every night before bed. I reveled
in the Bible's stories, which Grandfather Sims helped to
make understandable, the characters and details coming
alive for me, a child who hadn't yet learned to read.

In fact, I first learned to read by listening to this good
and godly man read from God's Word. It wasn't the books
about Dick and Jane and Spot the dog that taught me, but

instead a book about Abraham and Moses, David and Elijah, and most importantly, Jesus. Since then, I came to refer to the Bible as "the Jesus book."

With childlike faith I learned to love the Bible. And not only to love it, but to desire to live it so that I am not only a believer but a *doer* of the Word. God showed me in his Word how to live according to the truth. At the time I didn't know what a biblical worldview meant, but early on I began to see everything in life through the lens of Scripture, and that everything in Scripture is all about Jesus.

After the resurrection, Jesus' followers were walking home from Jerusalem on their way to a tiny village named Emmaus. Two men, or perhaps a married couple, were despondent because it appeared that the one they believed to be the Messiah was dead and gone, and with him their hopes and dreams for a better future. It seemed all was lost and buried in a borrowed tomb. Then the depressed disciples were joined by a man they didn't recognize. Though they didn't know it, they were being accompanied on their journey home by the risen Christ, and as the three walked together something marvelous happened. Knowing they were blinded by sorrow and grief, Jesus began talking with them through the Word.

"Beginning with Moses and all the Prophets, he [Jesus] interpreted to them in all the Scriptures the things concerning himself" (Luke 24:27). Can you imagine? The very one who authored his Word is here now explaining it? On the road to Emmaus, the two disciples had the privilege of hearing Jesus as he helped them to understand the meaning of the Bible. You might say that the Lord unlocked the mysteries of the Bible and enabled them to see why it was written. Jesus walked them through the Old Testament, from the creation to the great flood to the Ten Commandments, to the prophecies of Isaiah and Daniel to the Psalms and Proverbs. And as the risen Lord did this, he revealed himself. He stepped right out of the Bible and showed who he was and is: the Son of the living God. The Scriptures lived, and still live, because Jesus Christ lives.

With their faith restored and reignited, the disciples reflected on what happened when they met the Lord that day and walked with him. "They said to each other, 'Did not our hearts burn within us while he talked to us on the road, while he opened to us the Scriptures?'" (Luke 24:32). With hearts aflame, they ran back to Jerusalem and told the rest of the disciples that Jesus was alive. How did they know? Because they had walked with him in the Word!

The Bible is the Jesus book. He is the point of the Bible, both the Old and New Testaments. All of Scripture is about him and centers on him. It is his story, not just history. You will never understand the Bible until you know the Savior and experience his living presence in your life. Jesus is the living Word of God (John 1:14). This means God has spoken finally and fully and forever in the person of his Son. "Long ago, at many times and in many ways, God spoke to our fathers by the prophets, but in these last days he has spoken to us by his Son, whom he appointed the heir of all things, through whom also he created the world" (Hebrews 1:1–2).

A story has been told about former U.S. President Calvin Coolidge attending a church service without his wife, who was ill. Being a quiet man, Coolidge became known as "Silent Cal." After he returned home from church, the First

Lady asked her husband about the service. Silent Cal was unhelpful. He didn't remember the names of the hymns or what the choir had sung; he didn't recall if anyone had joined the church that day or who had prayed the prayers. Exasperated, Mrs. Coolidge asked what the sermon was about. "Sin," Silent Cal replied. "Well, what did the pastor say about it?" she asked. To which the president answered, "I think he is against it." He wasn't wrong, but when it comes to the Bible, may we pay more attention than he did.

We must not miss the message, for the Bible tells us who God is, what he is like, and how we can know him. As Francis Schaeffer once said, "God has spoken, and he is not silent." Yes, God has revealed himself and his Son, Jesus, and his Spirit has given the world a pure and perfect record of the story of salvation. So yes, the Bible is the Jesus book. It is not just a good book, but the book written so that we might know God and experience his love and life forever. The Bible is a living book, the breath of God is in it, and therefore we can live by its truth and trustworthiness all the days of our lives.

The purpose of Scripture is to present the person of the Savior. The Bible is the instrument of God to convey the message of Christ, and therefore the Bible should not be sought so much for its own sake but should be searched for the purpose of finding Christ. "To him all the prophets bear witness that everyone who believes in him receives forgiveness of sins through his name" (Acts 10:43).

Back to my boyhood: As a believer, the Bible has been my constant companion as I have walked with Jesus. But now, after all these years, I believe God's Word more than ever. I had the opportunity recently to visit Oxford, England,

and the renowned Oxford University Library. I made the trip with my two sons, Jason and Josh, along with biblical scholar and author Dr. Jeremiah Johnston, who serves as apologetics pastor of Prestonwood Baptist Church, where I serve as the senior pastor. Dr. Johnston secured an invitation for us to delve deep into the archives of the library, where we were shown the Jesus fragment—the most ancient of the New Testament manuscripts of the Gospel of Matthew. I held in my hand small pieces of the holy Scripture, written on parchment in Greek, the New Testament's original language. This parchment was old. Very old.

It was a wondrous moment for me as my mind flipped back to those early days when I sat with my grandfather and listened to God's Word being read aloud. Now, after all these years and life experiences, I can confidently say I believe the Bible more than ever. Holding that ancient manuscript in my hand reminded me of the impact God's Word has had on my life. His Word has lived in me from childhood until now, the seventy-something season of my life. I'm discovering each day the joy of the Lord as his Word penetrates my soul. The Jesus book has transformed my life, and my greatest privilege is to spend my day sharing his message of redemption. Join me in walking with Jesus through his Word and discover what it means to be his disciple. The same Word of God that changed me can change your life as well.

The Bible Matters Because the Bible Is Truth

The Bible and the story of Jesus transformed the world. The Bible is the number one bestselling book of all time. More copies have been printed in more languages and read by more people than any other book in history, and nothing else even comes close. Every day and especially on Sundays, it is read, studied, quoted, and preached in every nation and continent. The Bible has been translated into almost every language and is being translated into tribal languages and people groups in every nook and cranny of the planet to this day. Its unparalleled popularity would demand that we ask the question, Why? What is it about this ancient book, written between two and three thousand years ago, that makes it so loved still today in the twenty-first century? Why is the Bible believed, honored, and revered?

We call this book the Word of God and claim God wrote it. That is what sets the Bible apart from any other. When we speak of the holy Bible, the sacred Scriptures, we are referencing the very words of God.

I read of a scientist who held a human brain in his hand and reflected on what was inside it: the thoughts, the memories, the lifetime of learning and growing. It was amazing. When you hold a Bible in your hand, in one sense you're holding the mind of God, at least the part that he chose to reveal to us in words.

God has revealed himself to us in three main ways. The first is through creation: "The heavens declare the glory of God" (Psalm 19:1); the second is through the human conscience because the Spirit witnesses within us perfectly in Christ; and the third is that he has given us the Scriptures.

We use the word *inspiration* to describe how God wrote, and 2 Timothy 3:16 tells us that all Scripture is inspired and God-breathed. God's chosen human authors wrote down the words; however, this doesn't mean that the Bible was inspired simply due to its human authors. The Bible is holy and completely inspired because it is breathed out by God, it is his truth spoken to us, and it is 100 percent trustworthy. Another word we use to describe the Bible is *infallible*—that is, the Bible is wholly true in all that it says and can never make a mistake.

And then there's the word *inerrant*. I believe in the "verbal plenary inspiration" of the Bible—"verbal" meaning words, and "plenary" meaning the whole thing. Or as Southern Baptists have defined the Bible in their doctrinal statement, the Baptist Faith and Message: "The Bible is truth." It is without any mixture of errors; it is inerrant.

1   Why You Can Trust the Bible

Can you trust the Bible? That's a big question of great importance. The short answer is that yes, you can, because it was divinely inspired by the Holy Spirit, who continues to work in our lives through Scripture. But what does this mean, and how does it work?

When we read or we hear the Scripture, God speaks to us. He speaks to us through the ministry of the Holy Spirit, and he enlightens us to know the truth and empowers us to live out that truth. The Bible gives us doctrinal and historical truth, but it also gives us personal truth.

As we read or study Scripture, we can understand it better by asking these questions:

- What does this passage of Scripture mean?
- What did it mean then, when written?
- What does it mean now, today?

- What does it mean to me personally? In other words, how does this particular Scripture apply to my life?

The Holy Spirit illuminates his message to us. As it says in 1 Corinthians 2:9, "Eye has not seen, nor ear heard, nor have entered into the heart of man the things which God has prepared for those who love Him" (NKJV). Many people think this verse is about heaven and what we can imagine about the next life, but it's actually referring to what the Spirit says about the "now life." Through his inspired Word, God reveals to his children those things that are beyond our ability to see with the human eye. He shows us what we cannot see, hear, or imagine—that is, apart from divine revelation. This is the illuminating, enlightening ministry of the Holy Spirit. The Spirit works in our lives in many wonderful ways: counseling, correcting, enabling, empowering, interceding, protecting, and partnering with us in our witness.

Acts 1:8 says, "You will receive power when the Holy Spirit has come upon you, and you will be my witnesses. . . ." The Holy Spirit fills us and uses us as he imparts spiritual gifts to minister to others, and we can be assured the Spirit will move in us when we open our hearts to receive his Word. He shares God's truth in our hearts and minds, helping us to understand the Scriptures and apply it to our individual lives.

So when you open the Bible, ask God by his Spirit to open your heart. It is the role of the Holy Spirit to teach us. It is our responsibility to be teachable. Proverbs 1:23 says, "I will pour out my spirit to you; I will make my words known to you." This promise comes straight out of the Word of God, that not only do we have his Word, but we have his Spirit to make it known to us.

As a former athlete and now a fan of sports, especially baseball, I'm often amazed by the talent I see on the playing field today. These skilled athletes have developed their bodies and abilities to perform at the very highest levels, and a big reason for this is coachability. The greatest athletes are coachable, always wanting to improve in their sport and perform well. They listen to instruction and practice relentlessly under the guidance of a trained leader and teacher of the game.

I want to be a coachable Christian. This means I am always learning, growing, and exercising my spiritual muscles. As I have sought to be teachable over the years by studying the Scriptures, things that I have known for years have come alive to me in ways I can only describe as miraculous. This happens when I get reps in reading God's Word. The Spirit of God is showing me more and more light pouring out from his Word. I've read through the Bible many times, and the pages of Scripture are very familiar to me, yet the Bible always remains fresh as God speaks to my heart. Verses I've read and memorized throughout my life often speak to me in new ways. After all these years, I still feel as though I'm just beginning to grasp the meaning of Scripture. What is true for me is true for you because every believer possesses the Spirit, who is there to teach and guide us in our Christian walk. Let's always come to our time in God's Word with the prayer of the psalmist: "Open my eyes, that I may behold wondrous things out of your law" (Psalm 119:18).

George Müller, who in 1849 founded the Ashley Down orphanage in Bristol, England, once said, "The vigor of our spiritual life will be in exact proportion to the place held by the Bible in our life and thoughts." I've read the Bible through hundreds of times, always with increasing delight, and each time it seems like a new book to me. I look upon it as a lost day when I haven't taken the time to ponder the Word of God.

Many people hold the view that the Bible is hard to understand, and indeed there are deep truths in its pages that call for more patience, prayer, and meditation. In general, though, I've come to believe that the Bible is quite understandable when interpreted and illuminated by the Holy Spirit.

John MacArthur, Bible teacher and pastor, stated it this way: "It is my conviction that the Bible is not difficult for the believing heart to understand. And the more I understand, the more unshakable is my conviction that the Bible is the living, authoritative, inerrant Word of God. It has this remarkable effect on me. The more I study it, the more I hunger to know. God's Word, then, is not only the thing that satisfies my appetite, but it arouses an even deeper hunger for more. Sharing that hunger with others has always been the supreme joy of my heart as a pastor."[1]

Each book of the Bible was written at a specific time and place for a specific need at that time. God spoke to past generations long ago, and yet his Word is relevant today from generation to generation and will always remain so. The Scripture is timeless, speaking to our needs and the issues and challenges of our day.

Often the writers of Scripture wrote about future events they did not fully comprehend. This is what we call "prophecy," which is one of the miraculous features of the Bible. When these prophecies are fulfilled, it gives us yet another reason to believe the Bible and in the God who gave it to us. For example, when Isaiah penned the fifty-third chapter of the book that bears his name, he didn't understand the full meaning of the suffering of Jesus on the cross, something Isaiah described more than seven centuries before the pivotal event took place. The same could be said of Psalm 22, where the writer speaks of the death of Jesus as though he were standing at the foot of the cross.

And in the New Testament, we read, "As to this salvation, the prophets who prophesied of the grace that would come to you made careful searches and inquiries, seeking to know what person or time the Spirit of Christ within them was indicating as He predicted the sufferings of Christ and the glories to follow" (1 Peter 1:10–11 NASB).

How Reliable Are the Biblical Documents?

Both the quantity and the quality of the manuscripts of the Scriptures give us confidence in the Bible's accuracy. Although no original manuscripts of Old Testament books exist, scribes took painstaking efforts to preserve the Old Testament books by copying them by hand.

The Dead Sea Scrolls—discovered over a period of ten years, between 1946 and 1956—provide for us a Hebrew text that dates from the second century BC. Including all the Old Testament books except Esther, the Dead Sea

Scrolls confirm the reliability of ancient manuscript copies of the Old Testament.

Another important discovery was the pre-Christian Greek version of the Old Testament called the Septuagint, produced from about 285–270 BC. This version is frequently quoted in the New Testament because it served as the Bible of Greek-speaking Christians in the apostolic period. Scholars have also used this text to confirm the accuracy of Hebrew versions of the Old Testament.

When it comes to the New Testament, no book in ancient literature compares with the volume of ancient manuscripts still in existence. About 24,000 manuscripts exist: 5,664 in Greek; 8,000 to 10,000 in Latin; and 8,000 in Ethiopic, Slavic, and Armenian. In contrast, there are only 7 ancient copies of Plato's writings that still exist, 5 of Aristotle's, and 643 of Homer's. If we doubt what the New Testament manuscripts say about Jesus, then we must multiply those doubts a thousand times over for virtually any other classical literature and historical figure. And if we're to be this skeptical about the New Testament, we may as well throw out 99 percent of what we know about the ancient world because we cannot rely on any of the manuscripts and what they tell us about ancient times. Yet nobody is that skeptical.

The New Testament manuscripts are both numerous and ages-old. Approximately 75 papyrus fragments date from early AD 200 to mid-800, covering 25 of the 27 New Testament books. One fragment of the book of John has been dated as early as AD 100, which is only a couple of generations after the originals were written. At the same time, the oldest existing manuscripts of most non-biblical books date from eight to ten centuries after the original works were written. For example, the oldest manuscript of Caesar's Gallic Wars, composed between 58 and 56 BC, dates from about nine centuries after Caesar's day.

Thus the quality of the New Testament manuscripts is without parallel. Because of the reverence the early Christians had for the Scriptures, they exercised meticulous care in accurately copying and preserving the authentic texts. No discrepancies among the texts call into question a major doctrine or factual teaching.[2]

Unchanging Truth

God's Word is forever young and has no shelf life. This is because his truth is eternal. There will never be a need to update the Bible because its truth never changes. I read an article describing a social scientist's desire to consolidate all the major religions of the world into a new holy book that would be authored by artificial intelligence. That is, of course, preposterous. One cannot rewrite the Bible. If the intelligence it came from was "artificial," that would mean it was superficial, and the Bible is not superficial. It is supernatural.

The supernatural Scriptures are given by the supernatural Spirit of God. These words were alive in the millenniums before us and are still breathing life today. The writer of Hebrews claimed, "For the word of God is living and active, sharper than any two-edged sword, piercing to the division of soul and of spirit, of joints and of marrow, and discerning the thoughts and intentions of the heart" (Hebrews 4:12). I know this to be true in my own life because the Spirit of God speaks to me through his living Word when I prayerfully invite him to. So many times God has answered my questions, confronted my heart, calmed my soul, instructed my mind, and directed my path by way of his Word, the Scriptures.

God communicates to us personally, and his Word is relevant for every generation. After we are long gone and in heaven, his Word will live into the future for our children and their children and their children's children. It occurred to me a few years ago that it is unlikely my great-great-grandchildren will know my name or anything about me. I doubt you know the first and last names of your great-great-grandparents. Of course, this really doesn't matter. What is critical, however, is that those who come after us know Jesus, and that we carry our faith forward into the next generation and so on. When at last we all get to heaven, we will meet not only our predecessors, our parents from the past, but our children and their children in the future. This is because the Word of God endures from generation to generation. It is my prayer that our family will carry on the legacy of our faith. There is no other book like the Bible in that the Scriptures communicate spiritual truth to every generation.

The Bible also speaks to every culture in the world. No other book can make that claim. You may read an inspiring book of poetry, or a story of history, or an exciting novel, or even a great Christian book that strengthens and encourages you, but these books aren't able to reach across into all people groups and cultures the way God's Word can and does. Like God himself, his Word is alive and will remain alive forever. God's Word cannot cease to exist any more than God cannot cease to exist. "Heaven and earth will pass away," Jesus said, "but my words will not pass away" (Matthew 24:35). God's Word is powerful, able to penetrate the human heart. The Holy Spirit invigorates and illuminates living truth to every person who listens and believes.

I remember reading that the evangelist Billy Graham would sometimes struggle with the veracity of Scripture. He'd witnessed several of his classmates abandon their belief in God and the Bible as God's infallible Word. He wrestled with whether his faith was perhaps misplaced, naive, or uneducated. Recalling those doubt-filled days, Graham said this: "I believe it is not possible to understand everything in the Bible intellectually, but one day some years ago I decided to accept the Scripture by faith. There were problems I could not reason through. When I accepted the Bible as the authoritative Word of God by faith, I found immediately that it became a flame in my hand." Billy Graham preached to more people than anyone in the history of the world, all with the Bible in his hand and the Word of God on his lips.

Because I am a preacher, I depend on God's Word to do what only he can do when delivering a sermon. Nobody cares what I think about a subject. My opinions are irrelevant. When I stand up to preach, people want to know: Is there a word from God for me? What is God saying? What does the Bible say? This is the reason I preach and teach the Bible, praying the Holy Spirit will communicate to each person through me by the life-changing Word of God. It is futile to preach anything else but God's Word. Jesus warned the religious leaders that they were false teachers because they did not know the Scriptures nor the power of God (Matthew 22:29).

So let us preach and teach, reading and sharing God's Word while depending on his own dear Spirit to enable us to understand it.

2

The Big Picture of the Bible

As I mentioned in the last chapter, I've been studying, pondering, and reflecting on God's Word for many decades now. And my hope is that I will always crave this marvelous book of life. After all, it's the truth that transforms.

But what *is* the Bible? It's a complex book unlike any other, so it would be helpful to know how it's structured and for what purpose. The goal of this chapter is to set you on a course to understanding the big picture of the Bible. As you make your way through the Bible, it's important to realize the Bible isn't typically presented in chronological order, though you can read some editions of the Bible in chronological order that have been published for this very reason. Most Bibles, however, are laid out like sections of a newspaper. News stories are placed in one section, sports in another, business and finance in another, and so on. When you open a Bible, you will discover first the Old Testament, beginning with books of history from Genesis to Esther. Then comes a collection of poetry and wisdom literature from Job to Song of Solomon. A large section of the Old Testament consists of books of prophecy from Isaiah to Malachi.

The following table recaps how the various books of the Bible are organized:

The Bible Is an Inspired Library

The Old Testament (Hebrew Bible)

Historical Books	*Genesis – Esther*
Poetic Books	*Job – Psalms – Song of Solomon*
Prophetic Books	*Isaiah – Malachi*

The New Testament

The Gospels and Historical Growth of the Church	*Matthew – Acts*
The Letters or Epistles	*Romans – Jude*
Prophetic Book	*The Revelation*

God's Law and Where It Came From

Every July Americans celebrate the birthday of our nation. And if you paid attention in sixth grade history class, you will recall that the United States has a constitutional form of government. After long and rigorous debate, the framers and founders of our nation drafted the Constitution, which was delivered to representatives of thirteen federated states and then ratified as the official law of the land. The assumption that lies at the heart of our Constitution is this: The law is absolute. In other words, we're to be a nation not of leaders, but of laws. As a result, citizens of this nation have always been free to pursue the life of their choosing as long as those pursuits do not violate the laws of the land. Throughout this country's history, great prosperity has been brought to us, its people, and many would contend that this good fortune is due in part to the form of government that we've observed.

Similarly, just as the Constitution of the U.S. is the foundation on which our society rests, the Word of God, the Bible, in a much more noble and eternal sense, is the Constitution of the Christian faith. The Bible is the highest law of God and therefore the ultimate authority for all of life.

Just where did this law of God come from? In his book *Evidence That Demands a Verdict*, author and apologist Josh McDowell lists the various facts that figured into the origin of the Bible:[1]

- The Bible was written over a 1,500-year span covering more than 40 human generations.
- The Bible was written by more than 40 authors from every walk of life. They were fishermen, farmers, poets, preachers, shepherds, kings, tax collectors, scholars, military leaders, doctors, political officials, and more.
- The Bible was written in a host of different places on three different continents, i.e., Asia, Africa, and Europe.
- The Bible was written in three languages—Hebrew, Aramaic, and Greek—and from numerous perspectives, including history, law, poetry, didactic treatises, parable and allegory, biography, personal letters, memoirs, and prophecy.

- The Bible covers a multitude of subjects, many of which are considered controversial. Yet with all this diversity, each part of the Bible contributes individually to one unfolding story: God's marvelous love and his redemption of humankind.

How incredible it is that such a lengthy book could be written without collaboration by more than forty authors over a millennium and a half and yet could reflect a single theme and common agreement, even down to the most minute details? The obvious truth is that there has never been a book like the Bible, and there can be no accounting for the origin and continuity of the Bible outside of the supernatural.

Do you believe in miracles? I do. And one reason I believe in miracles is because when I hold my Bible, I am holding a miracle in my hands. The Bible is the supernatural, miraculous work and Word of God. The historical accuracy, the geographical accuracy, the fulfilled prophecies, the preservation of the texts, both Old and New Testaments, are all good reasons to trust the infallibility and inerrancy of God's Word. The Bible is the most scrutinized book in all the world, and yet no ancient manuscript of any kind is equal to its magnitude, to the preservation and integrity the Bible represents.

What the Bible Says about Itself

The Bible is an infallible ancient text and the inspired Word of God. According to 2 Timothy 3:16, the Scripture is "profitable for teaching, for reproof, for correction, and for training in righteousness." I like the way Bible teacher and author Warren Wiersbe speaks of this particular verse. In essence, he says that when the passage refers to teaching, it means the Bible is telling us what is right, and when it refers to reproof, what is not right. For correction, it's telling us how to get right; for training in righteousness, how to stay right.

God's Word not only restores our spiritual strength and sets our feet on the right path, but it helps us to stay on the course marked out for our Christian maturity. Knowing how the Bible came into existence is one thing; understanding why it's here is another matter altogether. And the best way to discover why it's here is to read what the Bible says about itself.

Perhaps no clearer picture can be found that concerns the distinctiveness and purposefulness of God's Word to humankind than the words of Isaiah 55:8–11. In this passage of Scripture, we read, "For my thoughts are not your thoughts, neither are your ways my ways, declares the LORD. For as the heavens are higher than the earth, so are my ways higher than your ways and my thoughts than your thoughts. For as the rain and the snow come down from heaven and do not return there but water the earth, making it bring forth and sprout, giving seed to the sower and bread to the eater, so shall my word be that goes out from my mouth; it shall not return to me empty, but it shall accomplish that which I purpose, and shall succeed in the thing for which I sent it." These verses give me incredible strength and confidence as a preacher of the gospel. What is true of me can be true for you. When we share the Word of God with others, we can count on the fact that God will send it forth for his own purpose and that his Word will fulfill that purpose every single time.

Regarding this passage in Isaiah, there are two things of special note or importance. First, the thoughts of God are different from the thoughts of human beings. To oversimplify, it's like a person who speaks only English being in the same room with a person who speaks only Mandarin Chinese. There can be precious little verbal communication between the two unless one learns the language of the other. In our case, it is an impossible proposition for humankind to learn the language of God, as God is holy or "other" than humankind. Truly we would be without knowledge of our Creator—that is, unless he came to us speaking our language, which is precisely what he did.

The Bible clearly shows the initiative God took on our behalf when he reached out to communicate with us at different times throughout human history. Hebrews 1:1–2 says, "Long ago, at many times and in many ways, God spoke to our fathers by the prophets, but in these last days he has spoken to us by his Son. . . ." Without question, these words of God were vital for the people who heard God speak firsthand at those various times. But what about the revelation of God's will to successive generations, including our own generation? It turns out, God had us in mind all along as well. This passage tells us that God chose to record a portion of what he spoke at various times and in various ways for the benefit of *all* people regardless of when or where they lived.

And so God revealed himself progressively as he spoke to us. Because God's thoughts and words are not our thoughts and words, he put his words into a permanent form by which they could be apprehended and comprehended, then applied across the ages and generations for the benefit of every human being who would be born on planet Earth.

The second thing of note in Isaiah 55:8–11 is that God's words carry a divine purpose. God doesn't send forth his Word arbitrarily, capriciously, or carelessly. Each and every word that comes from God serves a purpose in his overall plan, and those words come to us via his inspiration and personal direction. Christians may debate what certain passages in the Bible mean, but our lack of agreement with, or misunderstanding of, God's sentiments does not change what God meant or what he wants us to learn. When I consider God's spoken words, forever documented in the Bible, I think of a trumpeter in our church who accompanies our beautiful worship. Larry Brubaker can blow a horn! Just as Larry's breath exhales melodic notes, God too sounded a clear signal every time he played a series of written notes and breathed out the Scripture— note by note, word by word.

And just as our trumpeter arranges various notes to form a unified theme, God arranged the lives, personalities, attitudes, and capacity for understanding of each biblical author, so that the end result would be sweet to the reader's ear, making a clear and distinct sound as a musician brings the horn to life by blowing into it. God animated the authors of Scripture by breathing inspiration into and then through them, thereby conveying his message of redemption and grace to the whole of humankind. But there is more: Not only did God the Father testify to the truth of his Word, but so did the Son of God, the person of Jesus Christ.

The Bible through the Lens of Jesus

Jesus clearly and perfectly revealed God because he is God. Whether it's a company, a church, a service organization, a club, or a family, the flow of values and beliefs from the organization's leaders to its members ultimately determines the level of cohesiveness, harmony, and productivity. In the Church of Jesus Christ, there's no debate or discussion about who is the head of the Church. Jesus is our Lord, and we are members of his body. The living, growing organism we call the Church embodies Jesus' teachings. John 15:5 says that he is the vine, and we are the branches. He is the head, and we are the parts. He is the master, and we are the servants.

For instance, when was the last time your church debated whether or not we as Christ followers should love one another? When was the last time there was an all-church meeting to decide whether we should practice forgiveness? What about whether to practice kindness, patience, and peacemaking, or whether to take up the cross and follow Christ? We adhere to these principles because our leader is the Lord, and through his life experience and through the everlasting *Word of God* he has called us to follow him and to obey him.

Norman Geisler makes the case that Jesus authored, affirmed, and authorized the Old Testament. Our Lord said, "Do not think that I have come to abolish the Law or the Prophets; I have not come to abolish them but to fulfill them" (Matthew 5:17 NIV). Jesus tells us that the Old Testament is the Word of God, and it is relevant and extremely significant for Christians because he is the purpose of the Scriptures. When we approach the Bible with this essential truth in mind, everything begins to make sense. We then discover the spiritual principles for life in Christ today.

If you're reading the Bible and it doesn't make sense to you, start with Christ and your relationship with him. What could be missing is knowing the One of whom the Bible speaks, the One the Bible is all about. If you have no desire to read God's Word or take no delight in it, check your heart. Because if you want to know God, you will hunger for his Word. I've often said, *I don't know how much of God you have, but I know this—you have all you want.* Jesus said, "Blessed are those who hunger and thirst for righteousness, for they shall be satisfied" (Matthew 5:6). Our thirst is quenched, righteousness fulfilled as the Word of God penetrates our hearts through Christ our Lord.

Jesus, quoting the Old Testament, said, "Man shall not live by bread alone, but by every word that comes from the mouth of God" (Matthew 4:4). While in the upper room with his disciples, giving his last will and testament before the cross and the resurrection, Jesus said, "If you abide in me, and my words abide in you . . ." (John 15:7). This is the lasting legacy of our Lord. Blessed is the man or woman who hungers and thirsts for righteousness in Christ in God's Word. We know that God's Word is true and trustworthy, for the psalmist confirmed this when he said, "The law of the LORD is perfect . . ." (Psalm 19:7).

This is because God himself is perfect, and he can only speak what is perfect, pure, and blameless.

To the casual reader of the four Gospels, it can be easy to overlook that Jesus knew the Old Testament Scriptures from start to finish. And this despite not one mention of his having a copy of the law or the prophets' writings as he traveled throughout the land of Israel. Indeed, he couldn't have had a personal copy like we have our own copy today. Copies of the Scriptures were kept only in the synagogues. And yet as he spoke, the words of the Old Testament flowed from his lips with clarity and ease. From his younger years to adulthood, Jesus must have devoted significant time to the study and memorization of the Old Testament. We would do well to remind ourselves that when Jesus refers to or quotes the Old Testament in the four Gospels, he is doing so spontaneously and from memory.

From the beginning to the end of his life, Jesus' attitude toward the Word of God was one of submission to its authority. As a twelve-year-old boy, he astonished and astounded the Jewish teachers of the law in the Temple courts both by his questions and by his answers concerning the things of God.

At the outset of his public ministry, Jesus was led by the Spirit into a conflict with Satan. Jesus resisted all of Satan's temptations by submitting to the authority of the Word as it states in Luke 4:4. In fact, the phrase "It is written," or its counterpart "that the Scripture might be fulfilled," became the phrases the disciples heard more than any other. Consider the following verses: "Then Jesus said to them, 'You will all fall away because of me this night.

For it is written, 'I will strike the shepherd, and the sheep of the flock will be scattered'" (Matthew 26:31). "For the Son of Man goes as it is written of him, but woe to that man by whom the Son of Man is betrayed! It would have been better for that man if he had not been born" (Mark 14:21). "For I tell you that this Scripture must be fulfilled in me: 'And he was numbered with the transgressors.' For what is written about me has its fulfillment" (Luke 22:37). "I am not speaking of all of you; I know whom I have chosen. But the Scripture will be fulfilled, 'He who ate my bread has lifted his heel against me'" (John 13:18). "While I was with them, I kept them in your name, which you have given me. I have guarded them, and not one of them has been lost except the son of destruction, that the Scripture might be fulfilled" (John 17:12).

Shortly after Jesus was tempted by the devil in the wilderness, in a synagogue in Nazareth he revealed himself as the Messiah or the Anointed One to the Jewish leaders by reading and then applying to himself the messianic passage from Isaiah 61:1–2 (see Luke 4:14–21). Admittedly, he could have saved himself a measure of trouble by sitting quietly in the synagogue instead of acknowledging that he in fact was the long-awaited One, the Messiah. But whatever the cost, he knew he was there to obey the Word of God and teach what was true. Finally, he revealed that his earthly mission included suffering and even death by consistently pointing to the Old Testament prophecies about the suffering Messiah.

As a young man in his early thirties, humanly speaking, Jesus maintained an astonishing grasp of the Word of God and remained totally submissive to its authority.

Throughout his life, Christ seemed to be committed to two things: the will of his Father in heaven, and the authority of Scripture. In fact, Jesus saw them as inseparable, which they are. His submission to the authority of Scripture was the way he demonstrated his submission to the Father.

As mentioned earlier, in Matthew 5:17, Jesus says, "Do not think that I have come to abolish the Law or the Prophets; I have not come to abolish them but to fulfill them." He fulfilled what was written in Scripture with the same fidelity with which he fulfilled what his Father in heaven commanded him to do. He came to obey the Father's words, whether given to him directly or written in the pages of the Old Testament. Jesus understood that "Forever, O LORD, your word is firmly fixed in the heavens," as it's recorded in Psalm 119:89. The Word and the will of God are present tense, settled forever, and therefore Jesus never questioned them. Anyone who is a follower of Jesus can rest assured in this very same claim: The Bible is the authoritative Word of God.

Jesus' Acceptance of Old Testament Truths and Characters

There are many other examples that illustrate Jesus' confidence in the accuracy of Scripture. To begin with, he confirmed that Adam and Eve were literal people: "He answered, 'Have you not read that he who created them from the beginning made them male and female . . . ?'" (Matthew 19:4). He confirmed the story of Jonah and the great fish to be a literal occurrence: "For just as Jonah was three days and three nights in the belly of the great fish, so will the Son of Man be three days and three nights in the heart of the earth" (Matthew 12:40). He confirmed that Daniel the prophet wrote the book of Daniel: "The master of that servant will come on a day when he does not expect him and at an hour he does not know" (Matthew 24:50). He confirmed that Noah, the ark, and the great flood happened as recorded in the book of Genesis: "For as were the days of Noah, so will be the coming of the Son of Man. For as in those days before the flood they were eating and drinking, marrying and giving in marriage, until the day when Noah entered the ark . . ." (Matthew 24:37–38). He spoke of Sodom and Gomorrah as literal cities that were burned and buried under fire and brimstone from heaven: "But on the day that Lot went out of Sodom it rained fire and brimstone from heaven and destroyed them all" (Luke 17:29 NKJV).

Why was Jesus confidently appealing to biblical history, even making specific grammar choices, to convey truth? Because he knew that the verb tenses and types of nouns, as well as the historical record and accuracy of the Scriptures, were all inspired by his Father. He knew that God is in the details as much as he is in the broad brushstrokes of life.

You and I have a choice to make, and there are three options from which to choose. Number one, we choose to believe there are errors in the Bible that Jesus was unaware of, which would mean he was not all-knowing. Number two, we believe there are errors in the Bible stories, fables, and legends that Jesus knew about but didn't bother to share with us, which would bring into question his testimony, honesty and truthfulness. Or number three, we believe the Bible is indeed the Word of God and that it's 100 percent accurate without any mixture of error just as Jesus testified.

May you and I wisely choose the third option.

The Holy Spirit Declares the Truth of God's Word

It is not only by God the Father and God the Son that we receive testimony regarding the truth of the Bible. Because of the Holy Spirit in us, all those who have experienced the power of the Word of God in their lives can testify to the fact that the Bible is not just another book. Hebrews 4:12 tells us that the Word of God is alive. It is far more than dried ink on old paper. It is living and active, "sharper than any two-edged sword, piercing to the division of soul and of spirit, of joints and of marrow, and discerning the thoughts and intentions of the heart."

The Bible is to be demonstrated, not debated. Since it's true the Word of God is alive, you and I can have a fresh encounter with God each time we approach it. Reading, studying, and living in the truth of God's Word is unlike engaging with any other book on earth. When was the last time a history book saved your marriage, healed your wounded spirit, encouraged your teenage child, corrected a sinful habit in your life, or gave you courage and hope in the face of disease, despair, or even death? Unlike any other book, those people who embrace, consume, and surrender to the Word of God will be changed; they will be utterly transformed.

They are healed: "He sent out his word and healed them, and delivered them from their destruction" (Psalm 107:20).

They are convicted of sin: "For among them are those who creep into households and capture weak women, burdened with sins and led astray by various passions" (2 Timothy 3:6).

They are born again: "Since you have been born again, not of perishable seed but of imperishable, through the living and abiding word of God" (1 Peter 1:23).

They receive faith: "So faith comes from hearing, and hearing through the word of Christ" (Romans 10:17).

They increase in holiness: "That he might sanctify her, having cleansed her by the washing of water with the word" (Ephesians 5:26).

They are able to resist Satan: "And take the helmet of salvation, and the sword of the Spirit, which is the word of God" (Ephesians 6:17).

They are able to overcome the power of sin: "How can a young man keep his way pure? By guarding it according to your word" (Psalm 119:9).

They become faithful, stronger: "He is like a tree planted by streams of water that yields its fruit in its season, and its leaf does not wither. In all that he does, he prospers" (Psalm 1:3).

In other words, readers of God's Word will see their lives changed in an infinite number of ways, all because the Bible is not just a book but is the living Word of God given to save us and make us whole. If you want to be blessed in your life, beautifully and powerfully blessed, then peer into the Word of God, listen to the Word of God, and live out God's Word. Approach it as you would a relationship with a good friend: expectantly, enthusiastically, energetically, and excitedly.

You never know what you might discover or what God will supernaturally reveal to you when you open the marvelous pages of God's Word. This is the miracle of illumination. The Spirit of God enlightens us and energizes us with his very Word. The Bible is an inexhaustible storehouse of spiritual riches, wisdom, counsel, and truth, and it is yours to consume today.

Your First Steps as a Bible Reader

Since the days when I was a little boy sitting on my grandfather's knee, it has been my desire to know and live by the Word of God, and then to proclaim it to others. As Grandpa Sims read Bible stories out loud to me, my young mind understood even then that those utterances were more than average words. They were the words of life, God's words. Of course, it would take many more years before I fully grasped how truly set apart God's Word is, and with each step of the journey, I found myself more fulfilled. I pray that you will take the next step on this same journey. And to do so, you can begin by adopting the following three views as your own:

The Bible is authoritative. Submit yourself to it without reservation. Come with questions, but stay until you allow God to answer them. John 7:17 says, "If anyone's will is to do God's will, he will know whether the teaching is from God. . . ." Trust God to reveal his unique voice to you through his Word.

The Bible is authentic. Remember that if God inspired the Bible, then he inspired all of it, and so any part can speak to you. Each time you engage with the Bible, ask

God to show you what he would like for you to learn from the passage you're reading. In the words of Psalm 119:18, "Open my eyes, that I may behold wondrous things out of your law." Ask God to open your eyes as you read.

The Bible is accurate. Believe that if Jesus Christ trusted in the accuracy of all that is written in the Bible, you can rest assured that the Bible can withstand your scrutiny. Strive to be like the Bereans of old who studied the Scriptures daily to verify the accuracy of what the apostle Paul was teaching them. "Now these Jews were more noble than those in Thessalonica; they received the word with all eagerness, examining the Scriptures daily to see if these things were so" (Acts 17:11). If you come across something you don't understand or can't resolve, seek help from your pastor or from a good Bible study resource. Keep in mind that the Bible will reveal its treasures just as the earth reveals its gold and silver treasures to the diligent. According to Proverbs 2:3–5, "Yes, if you call out for insight and raise your voice for understanding, if you seek it like silver and search for it as for hidden treasures, then you will understand the fear of the LORD and find the knowledge of God." Make it your lifelong quest to prove to yourself what an amazing book the Bible is.

Welcome God's Word into your life as you would a beloved friend. In James 1:21, we read, "Therefore, put away all filthiness and rampant wickedness and receive with meekness the implanted word, which is able to save your souls." We welcome the Word of God because it is his truth by which we are made free. Some are in bondage, some have errant habits, some addictions, and those in chains wonder why. Jesus said in John 8:32, "You will know the truth, and the truth will set you free." The power of the Word of God will set you free from the bondage of sin and addiction and habits you can't conquer on your own. So it's by the power and truth of God's Word that we become truly free.

God's Words Are Seeds

I've never been much for working in the yard. My wife, Deb, would be the first to tell you that. But our son Jason, who is married and has a yard he is very proud of, is a gifted landscaper in ways that defy his genetics. One day, his wife, Toby, told me that Jason—wearing a hat, work clothes and gloves—reached for his wheelbarrow en route to the yard and said, "I'm about to go where no Graham male has ever gone before." Now, I'm not an expert on the whole sowing-and-reaping thing, but I do know that if you're going to grow a decent lawn, you first have to remove the weeds. This simple principle is one of God's favorite descriptions of his words. They are seeds in the hearts of every person alive.

In Matthew 13:3–9, Jesus tells a powerful story known as the Parable of the Sower: "A sower went out to sow. And as he sowed, some seeds fell along the path, and the birds came and devoured them. Other seeds fell on rocky ground, where they did not have much soil, and immediately they sprang up, since they had no depth of soil, but when the sun rose they were scorched. And since they had no root, they withered away. Other seeds fell among thorns, and the thorns grew up and choked them. Other seeds fell on good soil and produced grain, some a hundredfold, some sixty, some thirty. He who has ears, let him hear."

Just as seed produces life and fruit, so does the Word of God, which is why Jesus says, "Be very careful how you hear." It's a dangerous thing in many ways to hear the Word of God, a dangerous but marvelous thing. Jesus explains in his parable that some of the seed the farmer threw out landed on hard ground, and the seed could not penetrate the earth. Birds flew by and took the seed away. The hard ground represents the hearts of those who are unreceptive to the truth of God's Word. Fortunately, nobody has to live with a calloused heart because Jesus says there are other available responses to his Word.

The sower also sowed seed in the midst of the rocks. In the ancient world of Israel, topsoil was very thin. Limestone would peek through from underneath so that the seed couldn't effectively take root. The seed would go down a few inches and begin to sprout a plant, but as soon as the sun's rays shone down, the plant would wither and die. Jesus' point is that some people have a shallow heart, stony ground that cannot maintain good growth. Perhaps they respond initially to the Word of God, but six months later they're nowhere to be found in the kingdom of God. They allowed the seed into the top layer of soil, but they kept the Word from penetrating the deep recesses of their souls.

The farmer threw still more seed onto the ground, where thistles and briars chucked it out. The seed was overtaken by surrounding weeds—weeds of worldliness that stunt our growing in him. Whenever we allow our hearts to become distracted or divided by other interests, we lose our ability to welcome the Word of God into our lives. And God will not force his way in; he waits for you to welcome his Word of your own accord.

But there's a fourth situation the farmer encountered as he spread the seed. Jesus says there existed a certain amount of prepared soil, good soil that was ready to produce grain that would nourish life. This is to be the reality of our lives. When the Word of God gets planted deep inside of you, as the prophet Jeremiah said, it becomes your joy, the delight of your heart (Jeremiah 15:16).

God's Word becomes your oxygen, the most sustaining force in your life. It satisfies your deepest longings and the most profound needs of your soul. The Word provides strength amid our weakness, light in our darkest of nights. It is medicine to heal our wounds, a shelter in the raging storm. It is a fortress when we face the enemy; it is the truth with a capital T that beats down every lie. It is the Book of life. It is the Book of books. And it is ours.

My prayer is that we come to share the apostle Peter's posture regarding where ultimate truth for living is found: "Lord, to whom shall we go? You have the words of eternal life . . ." (John 6:68). Advertising makes bold claims about products that don't live up to the hype. Peter, on the other hand, makes a bold claim about God's Word that I promise will live up to your every expectation: "You have been born again, not of perishable seed but of imperishable, through the living and abiding word of God; for all flesh is like grass and all its glory like the flower of grass. The grass withers, and the flower falls, but the word of the Lord remains forever" (1 Peter 1:23–25).

Your Life Will Be Changed

Time spent in God's Word and prayer will change your heart, realigning it with his. Today most people spend countless hours watching negative and unproductive media, which serves to impair their spiritual health. Instead, go to God's Word to maximize the moment and allow your relationship with God to grow and flourish. When you meditate on God's numerous promises, you're built up and encouraged rather than weakened and deflated. When you seek God before you seek media, you will find peace and hope (see Matthew 6:33). Yet most of us do this in reverse. We check the news—CNN, the Drudge Report, etc.—before seeking God. As a result, we spend the day worried and worshiping the wrong things.

The Scripture tells us in 1 Timothy 4:8 that while physical training is good, training for godliness is much better, promising benefits in this life and the life to come. The same can be said of our minds. We must discipline them to dwell on good and pure things or they will lead us astray. No discipline is more vital in developing spiritual fitness than our time with God in his Word and in prayer. The Bible says in 2 Corinthians 4:16 that even if our outward body suffers wear and tear, inwardly we can be spiritually renewed by spending time with God. We need this time alone with God because the quality of our relationship with him determines the quality of every relationship we have in life. When we spend time with God, we are filled with his love, hope, and faith.

We'll go into the details of how to do this more later, but the important point is this: If you want to develop godly character and Christlikeness, then make taking some time to be alone with God the number one priority of your day. When you do, your life will be transformed. That includes your marriage, your family, your friendships, your work relationships, and every other person you come in contact with. Do your calendar and daily routine reflect spending time with God as your top priority?

3 What Is the Point of the Bible?

The story of the Bible can be described in one sentence. It's found in John 3:16, the familiar verse so many have read and memorized: "For God so loved the world, that he gave his only Son, that whoever believes in him should not perish but have eternal life." A well-known theologian was once asked, "What is the most profound thought that has ever entered your mind?" He answered by reciting the lyrics of the beloved hymn "Jesus Loves Me, This I Know" by Anna Bartlett Warner: "Jesus loves me, this I know, for the Bible tells me so. Little ones to him belong; they are weak, but he is strong. Yes, Jesus loves me! Yes, Jesus loves me! Yes, Jesus loves me! The Bible tells me so." In one simple song, we hear the love story of the Bible.

A friend of mine, Larry Shrier, was raised in a Jewish home. Because he didn't accept his faith as a young man, he went on a search for the meaning of life. He left his wife and began tramping across the United States, living in the back of his old car, just trying to figure things out. One day in North Carolina, while at the gas pump, something on the ground caught his attention. It was the remains of a gospel tract.

A gospel tract is typically the story of salvation written in a few words in a pamphlet. It is a witnessing tool. He picked it up and began reading it through. It was torn, blackened from tire treads, and smelled of gasoline. He could barely make out the words, but he began to read about Jesus and salvation. He thought, *I wonder what this is about. I need to know more.* So he took the dirty pamphlet into the service station and asked the attendant, "Can you tell me more about this?" The man said, "No, I can't. But there's a lady who lives down the street nearby. I think if you visited her, she could tell you more about Jesus. She talks about him all the time."

Minutes later, Larry knocked on the door of the lady's home. When she opened it, he held up the pamphlet and said, "I was told you could tell me what this is about."

She walked him through the Scriptures that were printed in the tract, explaining and introducing this young Jewish seeker to the Lord Jesus. He was more than interested. God's Spirit began to convict him. And over time, from just a few pieces of a gospel presentation lying on the ground at the service station, Larry asked Jesus to be his Messiah and Savior.

He wanted his estranged wife, Susan, to know what he had discovered and desired for her to experience the same glorious salvation. He also wanted to put their marriage back together. He thought she would never respond to him if he went home, so he sent her a telegram instead.

Remember those? In the telegram, he wrote, *Have come into a great inheritance. Contact me immediately.* That got her attention; she contacted him and welcomed him home. He explained to her what Jesus had done in his life, how Christ changed his heart. He was a new man and wanted to be the right kind of husband.

She watched and waited for a while, and she indeed saw the power of Jesus changing her husband's life. It wasn't long before Susan too received Jesus. She also had been raised in the Jewish tradition in New York, never really knowing who Jesus was. But now she met the Lord because of God's Word alive in her husband. It was an example of God's amazing grace! A few words of Scripture lying on the ground at a North Carolina filling station had changed a man's life, direction, destiny, marriage, family, and everything else about him.

Larry went on to be a minister of the gospel and served on our pastoral team at the First Baptist Church of West Palm Beach, where I served as pastor in the 1980s. To this day, Larry and Susan Shrier are serving the Lord as Christian counselors, and their children and grandchildren are Jesus followers. Their story illustrates the transforming power of God's Word.

The Bible is the only book that can change your life in such a profound way. Other books may entertain you, inspire you, and inform you, but the Bible can change you forever. Every page of God's Word is his supernatural, miraculous revelation, and every word of it is true. Within the Bible's pages we find life, faith, hope, love, meaning, and fulfillment, but more important, we find Jesus. Not only is the Bible transformative, but it is a treasure trove of truth. I pray that you develop a love and a heart of gratitude for your Bible, for it's the greatest, most valuable possession you own.

What Does the Bible Tell Us about Its Purpose?
Psalm 19:7–11 says,

> The law of the LORD is perfect, reviving the soul; the testimony of the LORD is sure, making wise the simple; the precepts of the LORD are right, rejoicing the heart; the commandment of the LORD is pure, enlightening the eyes; the fear of the LORD is clean, enduring forever; the rules of the LORD are true and righteous altogether. More to be desired are they than gold, even much fine gold; sweeter also than honey and drippings of the honeycomb. Moreover, by them is your servant warned; in keeping them there is great reward.

There are six synonyms in this passage describing the Scripture, which help us to understand what the Bible is and what God's Word accomplishes in our lives.

1. "The law of the Lord [Word of God] is perfect, reviving the soul." It is pure, it is righteous, and it will change you. The Bible is the source of life that points us to Jesus, our Savior and Redeemer who is "the way, and the truth, and the life" (John 14:6). The Bible alone contains the message of eternal life and salvation (1 Peter 1:3; John 20:31). We may know that God exists in creation, but we don't know how to come

into relationship with him apart from his Word. It's important to learn how to live out the Word of God, and that is what the Bible provides.

In the Bible we discover God's plan of salvation and how we can know and experience him, now and forever. This is true of both the Old and the New Testaments, for the two can't be separated. While some have suggested that we unhitch the Old Testament from the New Testament, that would be a huge mistake. There are 260 chapters in the New Testament, and only 12 of them don't include references to the Old Testament. From Genesis to Revelation, the Bible reveals to us how to enter the kingdom of heaven.

2. The second synonym in the Psalm 19 passage is in verse 7: "The testimony of the Lord is sure, making wise the simple." In other words, the Bible transforms our minds. The only way to change the way we live is to change the way we think. The Bible transforms the way we think. Romans 12:2 says, "Do not be conformed to this world, but be transformed by the renewal of your mind. . . ." This is your thinking regarding the Bible; it is living with a biblical outlook. It's how we view the world, humanity, marriage, family, morals, and life's meaning. This is called wisdom. We will begin to think more like Christ the more we get God's Word into our heads and hearts. And when you think like a Christian, you'll in turn act like a Christian.

3. "The precepts [or statutes] of the Lord are right, rejoicing the heart." This phrase tells us that the

Bible will transform our emotions. When you are down and discouraged and defeated in some way, the Bible is there to replenish, restore, and renew your joy. My good friend David Jeremiah—pastor, author, and Bible teacher—contracted a rare virus that attacked his spinal cord, and he was unable to walk for a period of time. But in the midst of a scary hospital stay and an arduous rehabilitation program, David remained full of joy. I asked him how he could remain so optimistic and upbeat, and he told me, as he was doing the physical work necessary to recover his ability to walk, he was memorizing the book of Philippians. This book is known as "the joy book." Despite his pain and disability, David Jeremiah was praising God because of his Word. The rejoicing of the heart through God's Word turns pain into praise. It is medicine for the soul. The Bible is not only good theology, God's theology, but it is good psychology. Jeremiah 15:16 says, "Your words were found, and I ate them, and your words became to me a joy and the delight of my heart, for I am called by your name, O Lord, God of hosts."

4. "The commandment of the Lord is pure, enlightening the eyes." Next, the Bible transforms our vision. We see life through a different lens. Psalm 119:105 says, "Your word is a lamp to my feet and a light to my path." We begin to see things the way God sees things, which again signifies wisdom. I define wisdom as seeing things from God's perspective. When you can't see your way through and are facing a time of

darkness with questions you don't know the answers to, God's Word is a light and a clear direction amid the darkness. In his Word, you'll begin to see God at work in you and in the world at large.

5. "The fear of the Lord is clean, enduring forever." Next, the Bible transforms our future. In a world where everything is constantly changing, we need something that doesn't change, something that lasts. God's Word is not only real, but it is relevant to every generation. The Word of our God stands forever. Psalm 19:9 says the Bible transforms our doubts and fears into faith and fortitude because it is true and righteous. In this life, there aren't many things that are absolutely true and just. How can we know what to believe and who to believe? Many people today have lost trust in our major institutions—government, education, media, even the church. As a pastor I often hear people say, "I don't know what to believe these days." Doubts and fears arise. Some even add, "I don't believe anymore at all." But you can trust the Bible and stake your life on it. It has proven itself over and over again, and its truth is absolute and unchanging, just like Jesus Christ who "is the same yesterday and today and forever" (Hebrews 13:8).

In our generation, we must earnestly contend for the faith (Jude 3). The Bible will transform our values. It is your vision that produces your values in life. Psalm 19:10 says that God's Word is more valuable than possessions and better than any profit. We follow the stock market and devour entertainment and chase after money, but what we really need to do is to chase after God's Word because in it is pure gold, the greatest possession of life and better than anything money can buy. The Bible is a spiritual inheritance for you and your children, which will produce a lasting legacy in your life and family.

6. "The rules [or judgments] of the Lord are true and righteous altogether." The Bible will transform our behavior. This is a warning to protect us from sin and its consequences. This is why it is so important that we declare the whole counsel of God when we preach or teach the Bible, not in anger but in love. "Speak the truth in love" is a commandment found in Ephesians 4:15. God's Word may be offensive to the world, but it pleases God when we take him at his Word in matters of right and wrong. As the old saying goes, "The Bible says it, I believe it, and that settles it." But I've learned to say instead, "The Bible says it, and that settles it whether I believe it or not!" So let's choose to believe what God says because God's Word is always true. God will reward our trust and obedience to his Word. This is why we keep believing. We keep reading, memorizing, studying, obeying, teaching, preaching, sharing God's Word. I intend to do this until my last breath (Psalm 56:11).

The Joy of Trusting God's Word

Take God at his Word. We can take him at his Word because he is true and faithful. No matter our circumstances or how we feel, we can live in the calm assurance that his love is faithful, and he keeps every single one of his promises. There are hundreds of promises in the Bible, and if you are a follower of Jesus, each one has your name on it. His promises address every need you may have, every battle you may fight, every circumstance you may face, and every burden you may bear.

We should live by what we know, not by how we feel, and here's what we know: God is good, God is faithful, and God is able to keep all of his promises to us. "For all the promises of God find their Yes in him . . . it is through him that we utter our Amen to God for his glory" (2 Corinthians 1:20). Which is another way of saying we can count on his promises. They are guaranteed by the cross and the resurrection of Jesus. God cannot and will not lie or invalidate any of his promises to his children. The Bible says that "he who promised is faithful" (Hebrews 10:23), and this is the reason we can live with hope and hold on to hope every day of our lives. Hope is the calm assurance of knowing our future is in God's hands. Let us then hold unswervingly to the hope we profess.

One of my favorite hymns is "Great Is Thy Faithfulness." It was written by Thomas Chisholm, who was a farmer, a publisher, and a preacher. At the age of fifty-seven, he read the third chapter of Lamentations and wrote a poem about it, which later became one of the best hymns ever composed:

> Great is Thy faithfulness, O God my Father;
> there is no shadow of turning with Thee;
> Thou changest not, Thy compassions, they fail not;
> as Thou hast been, Thou forever wilt be.

Great is Thy faithfulness!
Great is Thy faithfulness!
Morning by morning new mercies I see;
all I have needed Thy hand hath provided:
great is Thy faithfulness, Lord, unto me!

Summer and winter, and springtime and harvest;
sun, moon, and stars in their courses above
join with all nature in manifold witness
to Thy great faithfulness, mercy, and love.

Pardon for sin and a peace that endureth,
Thine own dear presence to cheer and to guide;
Strength for today and bright hope for tomorrow:
blessings all mine, with ten thousand beside!

I love the phrase "strength for today and bright hope for tomorrow." At our church in North Texas, one of the well-known voices and personalities of our congregation is Michelle Aguilar Whitehead. She directs social media and is often seen on camera. As her countenance beautifully reflects and radiates Christ, she welcomes our online congregation and invites them to worship. Several years ago, Michelle won the contest on the reality TV show *The Biggest Loser* by shedding 110 pounds, earning herself a quarter of a million dollars in prize winnings. When she returned home after the taping, before the show aired, a friend said to her, "You know, I never saw you as someone who was overweight. You're just Michelle. I just see you. I don't see anyone else."

To Michelle that was a great encouragement. She told journalists Lee Maria and Colette, "A huge lesson that weight loss taught me was we think everyone sees our flaws, but really they see you. They see who you are as a friend, a wife, a mother, a sister. They see who you are, not what you are. The scale wants to tell you who you are. It's a great way to check in and keep you accountable, but it is only a tool. It doesn't define who you are."

Michelle said that with her physical health and in her roles as wife and mother, she relied on God's Word every step of the way. She said trusting God made all the difference in the world. She went on to say, "For me I could not have done *The Biggest Loser* or be the wife and mom I am today without my relationship with Jesus."

When you live according to God's Word and trust him and his faithfulness in your life, he will give you great joy and happiness in the journey. Michelle is such a radiant Christian because she's reflecting the love and faithfulness of God in her life. We discover in the Bible that we aren't who we think we are or what the world says we are, but we are who God says we are (Psalm 145:13–14, 17). The Lord is trustworthy in all he promises and faithful in all he does. The Lord upholds all who fall and lifts up all who are bowed down. The Lord is righteous in all his ways.

When you begin your day with God and his Word— praying, meditating, and worshiping him—it changes everything, including how you live your day. You can then live with expectancy, excitement, and enthusiasm. The Bible, God's Word, will fill every day with wonder, joy, and optimism. You will never be the same as Jesus transforms the way you live.

4 Reading the Bible as a Lens to See the World

America is experiencing an existential crisis of belief, but I believe the source of the challenge is different from what many people may think. It is not an economic challenge, or a border challenge, or a law-enforcement challenge, or a healthcare challenge. With suicide rates at an all-time high in my lifetime[1] (and the Church is not immune to this), and with global conflicts in Europe and the Middle East, the world in many ways seems to be at a tipping point.

But what is the cause of the crisis? It is that we've shifted our dominant worldview. Every decision that every person makes every moment of every day of their life is based on their worldview, and when you shift your worldview, you're naturally going to get different outcomes. We tend to treat only the symptoms rather than the cause of the crisis, ignoring the worldview shift that is at the root.

What Is a Worldview?

A worldview is the decision-making filter we use every day. This affects how we process information intellectually, emotionally, and spiritually. Based on this worldview processing, we generate decisions and make hundreds of choices in a single day. Our worldview influences every decision we make.

So the question is not "Do I have a worldview?" (you do, even if you don't realize it), but rather "What worldview do I have?" Your worldview is what helps you determine right from wrong, good from bad, appropriate from inappropriate. It helps you figure out what kind of a person you want to be, how you want to be seen by others, what kind of reputation you want to have, what kind of legacy you want to leave, and what impact you want to make on the lives of those around you.

The agnostic skeptic Immanuel Kant (1724–1804), an Enlightenment thinker, first coined the term *worldview*, which comes from the German *Weltanschauung*. *Welt* means "world," and *Anschauung* means "point of view," "opinion," or "perception." From the perspective of a follower of Jesus, not just any worldview will do—we need to have a biblical worldview. A biblical worldview essentially declares:

> Every decision I make, I'm going to filter through my knowledge and understanding and interpretation of what the Bible says because the Bible is absolute moral truth. The Bible is God's guide on how to live a successful, thriving life.

At Prestonwood Baptist Church, our apologetics pastor, Dr. Jeremiah Johnston, and I prayerfully created the following definition and explanation about what we mean when referring to a biblical worldview:

> A biblical worldview is Scripture- and Jesus-centric, which means orienting the values, decisions, and priorities of our lives around the center of that worldview—Jesus Christ as Lord and Savior as revealed in the unchanging Word of God.

What Does It Mean to Live with a Biblical Worldview?

Living with a biblical worldview allows us to be true disciples of Jesus Christ by enabling us to think like Jesus so that we can live like Jesus. You live knowing God made you on purpose and for a purpose, and this changes everything. Arthur Holmes (1924–2011) was a longtime philosophy and English literature professor at Wheaton College in Illinois. Few have given more thought to Christian education and the Christian worldview.[2] Over one hundred of Professor Holmes's students went on to earn doctoral degrees, with many of his former students pursuing advanced study in such fields as history, literature, and biblical studies. Wheaton College President Philip Ryken said, "It would be hard to think of anyone who has had a greater impact on Christian higher education than Arthur Holmes." I would agree. In Dr. Holmes's book *Faith Seeks Understanding*, and in his book *All Truth Is God's Truth* published a few years later, Professor Holmes makes the point that Christian faith and truth must go hand in hand.

Christian faith is not, and should never be, in conflict with truth.

The God of Christian faith is a God of truth. He is not a God of error or falsehood. We humans are fallible creatures who must learn and be taught from what God has revealed in his Word and in his world. The one helps us to understand the other. Just as surely as we don't possess all that is known with respect to the world, neither do we fully comprehend all that's known with respect to the Word of God. Both must be studied with an open, honest mind. In other words, our education is vital.

Professor Holmes helped faculty and students alike think carefully about the Christian worldview, integration, and what they meant. What he pointed out is that many Christian teachers and faculty viewed integration as a mingling of the secular and the sacred, or in some cases "Christianizing" a theory or perspective that at its core was seriously at variance with Christian truth and values.

Integration, Professor Holmes explained, is not mixing secular thinking (whatever ideas happen to be in vogue) with lasting truth; rather, integration requires a thorough evaluation of everything we think and believe, from assumptions to methods. Only then can a Christian worldview worthy of the name emerge.

Being Human Is Not Exclusively Biology

When it comes to having a biblical worldview, let's start with the question of who we are as people. Can we describe the full measure of a human being if we limit our knowledge to the brute facts of biology? If who we are as humans fails to consider our spiritual and moral dimensions, will we truly discover the essence of who we are? Dr. Jeremiah Johnston probed this important question in his book *Unimaginable: What Our World Would Be Like Without Christianity* in which he describes the horrors that overtook the world in the twentieth century when anti-Christian and anti-God worldviews dominated the social and political landscapes of several countries—when the philosophies of men like Friedrich Nietzsche and Karl Marx inspired men like Adolf Hitler and Joseph Stalin. Embracing a new worldview that declared God was no more, these men sought to erase humanity too. No longer made in the image of God, humanity could now be treated like two-legged animals. Unwanted humans were rounded up and enslaved, and millions were murdered.[3]

I mention these atrocities only to underscore the point that *thoughts matter*. A person's worldview is not of little consequence. Today our society is in the middle of a great struggle between two competing and often diametrically opposed worldviews: One is the worldview that has dominated the West for centuries and in the last two hundred years has made inroads into the East. That is the worldview of Christianity, a worldview that says the universe was made by an intelligent, loving Creator. It is a worldview that offers the best explanation for the ongoing discoveries of science. This worldview affirms that humanity is made in the image of God and therefore human life is precious, that it has purpose and a destiny.

But this Christian worldview is being pushed aside by an increasingly hostile alternative worldview, a worldview that says there is no God and that we humans have no real purpose, that we are nothing more than a cosmic accident; that we have no future and no destiny, that ultimately our future is oblivion. This is the philosophy of nihilism, which comes from the Latin word *nihil*, which means "nothing." The nihilists claim there is no ultimate truth, there is no right or wrong, there are no morals, there is no God, that we humans are not especially important, and that someday the human race will become extinct. This will be the end. Game over.

I'm not making this up, and this is not just my take on things. It is what Oxford biologist Richard Dawkins, one of the most famous atheists in the world, has in fact declared: "The universe we observe has precisely the properties we should expect if there is, at bottom, no design, no purpose, no evil and no good, nothing but blind, pitiless indifference."[4]

Jeremiah, my church's director of apologetics I mentioned earlier, used to teach at Acadia Divinity College, which is part of Acadia University, located in eastern Canada. Acadia University is elite, like the Canadian Ivy League. On one occasion, Acadia University professor of philosophy and atheist Paul Abela presented a lecture he called "The Struggle for Meaning." In this lecture he asserted that life had no meaning, that life was hardly more than an agonizing struggle with unending pain, sickness, and weakness. He said, "If we could hear all of the world's insects and animals, it would be a never-ending scream."

Professor Abela could see nothing in the world that gave him hope. Humanity was just an unfortunate biological accident, and someday it will end. Can you imagine a worldview more dismal than that? I feel sorry for Professor

Abela. What hope can he share with his family, with his students? None. Is it any wonder that suicide among today's youth is on the rise? Many young people simply have no hope because they have embraced a worldview that is pessimistic—or worse, it is nihilistic. They feel there is *nothing* to live for.

The Christian Worldview and Character

Returning to the deep-thinking Professor Holmes, I believe he was years ahead of his time. Thirty-five years ago, he was able to discern where our increasingly secular society and its increasingly nihilistic educators were going. It seems we have finally arrived, and the end result is troubling.

How do we construct a healthy Christian worldview? It begins with our minds and how we think. Faith and the mind are not at odds; faith is not believing nonsense or embracing unreasonable, illogical things. In short, faith is not stupid. Some people seem to have faith in faith, as Dawkins and other atheists have pointed out. But true faith is intelligent, it is educated, and it is hungry for understanding. A healthy faith is a seeking faith. A healthy faith is not satisfied with remaining ignorant, naive, in the dark.

There's a moral side to the Christian worldview as well. Faith and knowledge are not value neutral. Morals have a lot to do with how we learn and what we do with what we learn. It may shock you to learn how many prominent thinkers and intellectuals in the twentieth century perverted their own research. They misrepresented their findings, distorting their research and conclusions because they didn't want to explore anything that challenged their preferred morals.

In Paul Johnson's book *Intellectuals*, he gives example after example showing how people like Bertrand Russell and Jean-Paul Sartre were dishonest and immoral, their philosophies and behavior untethered to right and wrong. Even worse are the findings of Michael Jones. In his book *Degenerate Moderns* (1993), he catalogs a veritable rogues' gallery of academic cheats like Sigmund Freud, Margaret Mead, and Alfred Kinsey, who rigged their research to produce results that were compatible with their depravity. Aldous Huxley, poster boy of the age of atheism and moral-free secular society, candidly admitted that people like himself and the aforementioned weren't interested in discovering truth, for they didn't care to find anything that contradicted their moral preferences and view of the world.

There really can be no Christian worldview, no authentic quest for truth, no deep and satisfying knowledge if there are no morals, if there is no character. The disturbing studies of Paul Johnson and Michael Jones have made that truth all too clear. Having a working worldview isn't just a matter of intelligence or an accumulation of facts; ultimately it is a question of character. Education, truth, knowledge, and character are the essential building blocks of a Christian worldview.

Whose Job Is It Anyway?

Let's close this chapter by considering who's responsible for a Christian or biblical worldview. According to the

Bible, it is the parents who have the primary responsibility of shaping the beliefs of their children. But it's the community of faith (the local church) that is responsible for helping equip and support parents in the process of developing this biblical worldview.

Which is why we must develop strategies with our churches and within our families for the biblical, systematic, comprehensive, and intentional teaching of our children, youth, and families surrounding a biblical worldview. The beauty of Romans 12:1–2 reminds us that our worldview must change to match the Bible. And this doesn't happen automatically for the believer, but through intentionality. The goal with regard to Romans 12:1–2 is for every believer to have a confident, well-rounded biblical worldview. I pray you too share this desire to develop a biblical worldview.

5 Reading the Bible for Hope and Reassurance

Not long ago, I visited a woman who was facing the end of her walk on this earth. Despite the uncertainty and confusion that accompany imminent death, she seemed strangely serene and completely devoid of fear. I asked her about her confidence, her optimistic outlook, her undeniable sense of peace. She replied, "I'm resting on the Word of God—his comforting, holy Word."

In this chapter I want to make the case that there's no better book to live by, and no better book to die by. There certainly is no better book than the Bible in which to look for life and its true meaning. If the Bible isn't true, then any old book would do. But if God's Word is sure, if it is settled, this ushers in "strength for today and bright hope for tomorrow," as the great hymn assures us. There's only one book in existence that supernaturally points us to life and love in Jesus Christ, and that book is God's holy Word.

Years ago, in an episode of the TV talk show *Larry King Live*, a five-member panel made up of ministers was offering their thoughts on the subject of God and war. And while I think it's completely appropriate for Christians to respond to the issues of war and peace in our times, I believe those responses must be rooted in something other than personal opinion or political preference. This can be said, of course, of many issues of our times. I was amazed as I listened to several of the members of the panel express beliefs that had no basis whatsoever in the Bible.

I go to the Word of God when I'm facing the imponderable and inexplicable questions of life that creep in from time to time. Some of these questions are personal, such as when someone is facing death, like the woman I mentioned above. Some of those questions are political or even global, like the questions the ministers on *Larry King Live* discussed. But either way, the Bible is a powerful source of wisdom and reassurance. When there's war, when there's death, when there's tragedy, when there's a cancer diagnosis, when there's a terrible accident and we don't understand where to look for help and understanding, we must turn to the Word of God.

One of the best things I did as a young Christian was to begin memorizing Scripture. Not only did the practice help keep and cleanse me from sin, but it has been a tremendous source of comfort. As I have visited with brokenhearted believers in hospital rooms, funeral chapels, and intensive care units, I've seen God's Word bring healing and hope to those who are crushed in spirit. I've seen their faith strengthened and deepened because God speaks to and enables Christians to overcome crises and live on in the power and promises of God. "Weeping may endure for a night, but joy comes in the morning" (Psalm 30:5 NKJV).

Simon Peter spoke of the Scriptures as being the word of prophecy, and that's comforting to know when we fear what's happening around us. The Bible brings a sure word about the future as well as the present. With so much anxiety and fear about what's coming next in the world, it's wonderful to remember that as Christians, we have a hope and a future. How do we know this? Because the Bible tells us, "For I know the plans I have for you, declares the LORD, plans for welfare and not for evil, to give you a future and a hope" (Jeremiah 29:11). If you're looking for stability in uncertain times, as you consider your future, turn to your Bible.

At least one fourth of the Bible was prophecy when it was written, and while much of it has already been fulfilled, there is much more yet to unfold. The only sure word concerning what's to come is found in the Word of God. This is where we find real hope. Whether that is the future of the world or your own personal future, the Bible will help you understand the times and help you live with assurance instead of anxiety and fear. You will live in peace, not in panic. But with so many opinions and speculations around us, how can we know what is true?

Leaning on the Only Book You Can Trust

If you're paying attention to the news media or the latest predictions on the internet, you may feel confused. Most people don't trust the media, and for good reason. When Peter wrote of the sure Word of God, the Church was surrounded by the lies of false teachers who were denying the truth of Scripture. In fact, Peter wrote a letter—which we now call the book of 2 Peter—to expose these lies as well as the false teachers spreading the lies.

The way to expose a counterfeit bill is to compare it carefully with a real one, and the way to expose a lie is to compare it with the truth. We must know God's Word to discern what is true and what is untrue, what is right and what is wrong. When you survey the opinions of people in our present-day culture, even those within the Church, you'll discover a startling sense of confusion about what is true—among believers as well as unbelievers.

God has clearly spoken through his Word, and as Christians we must fully embrace this fact. The Bible has been under attack in every generation through the centuries, not just our own. There's always been a battle over the Bible, and this war began in the Garden of Eden when Satan, disguised in the form of a serpent, questioned God's Word. When the serpent said to Eve, "Did God actually say . . . ?" (Genesis 3:1), he placed a question mark on the Word of God.

I first became alert to this spiritual battle for the Bible as a young Christian. As a college student, I soon realized not everyone believed the Bible as I did, and so my faith was being challenged beginning with the nature and authority of the Scriptures. The truths I had learned as a child needed to mature. I needed to know what I believed and why I believed it. Why should we accept that a book is really God's Word? How do we know we have an accurate text and translation of Scripture? Are there errors in the Bible? Is the Bible a trustworthy guide to life on questions of salvation, eternity, pain and suffering, morality, relationships, and hundreds of other issues we must face? Can I prove the Bible to be true? These are all questions every serious Christian should ask themself. We should be thinking Christians, "always being prepared to make a defense to anyone who asks you for a reason for the hope that is in you . . ." (1 Peter 3:15).

As we've discussed in earlier chapters, thankfully there's solid evidence for the Bible's unique position as God's book, that God himself actually wrote the Bible. I'm convinced that the Bible, all of it, is the living, breathing, eternal, supernatural revelation of God. That's the first thing we must be sure of before we can be comforted and reassured by its words. As a young preacher, this became fundamental to my calling, to contend for the faith once delivered (Jude 3). I learned you can indeed trust the Bible in a world of unbelief, and that I could count on its truth to lead me through life.

My Own Dark Night

In my sophomore year of college, I met and married a beautiful girl named Deb. We fell in love immediately, were married as students, and began our life together in the summer of 1970. I was preaching all over West Texas as a youth evangelist, and Deb often traveled with me to sing and play the piano. With my Bible in hand, I preached my heart out at youth revivals and rallies in small towns and churches all over Texas, never imagining what was about to happen to our family.

At the end of a hot August, while preaching and evangelizing at a little place called Crowell, Texas, my older preacher brother, Bob Graham, called to deliver terrible news. Our father, Tom Graham, had been mortally wounded at his hardware store in Fort Worth. A thief had attacked my dad with a claw hammer and beat him with multiple blows to the head. The father I loved was left unconscious and died ten days later.

Our family was devastated by his tragic death. We were cast into the fires of suffering and sorrow. My faith was also in that fire. But God was with us, and we all were comforted by the God of all comfort. Still, the tragic event was definitely a major test of faith. It's been said that the faith that can't be tested is a faith that can't be trusted.

The day after my dad's death, my pastor called to express his care and concern for me and our family. Dr. Fred Swank was a wonderful shepherd and leader who had grounded me in God's Word and had just that same year ordained me and my lifelong friend, O. S. Hawkins, to the gospel ministry. Most of the words he said that day are long forgotten, but the Scripture he shared, one that I had never heard or noticed until that time, is still with me. "Be merciful to me, O God, be merciful to me, for in you my soul takes refuge; in the shadow of your wings I will take refuge, till the storms of destruction pass by" (Psalm 57:1).

I was just twenty years old and facing the trial of my life. I was a Bible-believing preacher, but now I needed to know that God's Word was true. The words of Psalm 57 forever echo in my mind. It's a Scripture I have repeated to hundreds and hundreds of hurting people through the years. When we have questions we can't answer, doubts and fears we can't shake, pain that pierces the heart, God's Word can be trusted to calm and comfort us. It is a sure word that settles the troubled soul and brings healing to the broken heart.

One day Jesus spoke hard words to a large crowd of seekers, men and women who had been miraculously fed with a few loaves and fishes. When the Lord challenged them with the demands of discipleship, many of them turned and walked away, rejecting him. Jesus then asked his twelve disciples, "'Do you want to go away as well?' Simon Peter answered him, 'Lord, to whom shall we go? You have the words of eternal life . . .'" (John 6:66–69). Jesus not only possesses the words of eternal life, but he *is* the Word of Life.

The Bible provides the eternal words that offer life to all who believe and follow Jesus. What I determined to do in those dark days was to keep believing the Bible and not throw away my faith, but instead by God's grace dig deeper into the Bible and trust his Word in the darkness. By knowing him more and more, I stayed with Jesus and walked with him in the Word. Where else would I go?

We need to learn to take God at his Word and trust what he says. When we believe God's Word, trusting him to do what he promises, we can expect him to act. Taking God at his Word means that we believe it and we receive it. We "welcome the word," as the book of James tells us, and then God acts in ways only he can. The British preacher Charles Spurgeon called the Bible "faith's checkbook," saying that "All the riches and resources of the heavenly bank are available to us in Christ and guaranteed in God's

Word so that the Bible is a window in which we look and see our Lord."

I don't want to pretend that one Bible verse makes all the pain go away. But if we lean on his Word and his Spirit, day after day, it will give us the strength we need to carry on. The year 1970 was a tipping point for me, and in more ways than just my father's untimely death. I was ordained by my home church as a minister of the gospel, which marked my official starting point in the ministry.

I was called to be the pastor of a small church, The Eastside Baptist Church of Cross Plains, Texas, preaching twice every Sunday and serving the 25–30 members. In the spring of that same year, I was involved in a car accident that totaled my 1962 Rambler. It was my first car, which I'd bought for ninety dollars—not much of a loss, but it was the only car I had. Deb and I were married on May 22 of that year, 1970, and we began our first summer together with me preaching all over Texas at youth revivals. Then came August 18, the day my father was murdered. How could I carry on with life and ministry after that? The idyllic happiness of that first summer of marriage, preaching the gospel as a traveling evangelist, and the excitement of a young preacher were all shattered.

At age twenty I was facing deep sorrow for the first time in my life. The grief, coupled with the anger over my dad's brutal murder, was overwhelming. My mother was now a young widow, and our family was broken. After my father's funeral, Deb and I returned to our little rental house on the campus of Hardin Simmons, and life began again as a student. Now a married student, I was grieving but still believing God's Word and pursuing my calling as a minister. The Spirit of God comforted me in the most unimaginable ways in this most unimaginable loss.

Day in and day out, God's Word gave me the strength to continue, and even today it motivates me to keep going. It still hurts to remember those horrific days of grief, but the scars that remain on my soul remind me of God's grace, the hope I have in Jesus, and how I learned all of this in his book, the Bible.

And so can you. No matter what you may face in life, God's Word by his Spirit will strengthen you to move forward and never, ever give up. We as believers and followers of Jesus, based on what God's Word says, should not be afraid to go forward. God will give us the courage to do so. We know that the Word of God cannot lie and does not contain a single word that is incorrect or misleading.

6 Reading the Bible Daily

One of the most powerful and persuasive ways to defend your faith and witness to the gospel is by sharing your personal experience and testimony. This is bigger than theory, opinion, or speculation, but instead is a faith built on what God has done in your own life founded on God's Word. It is the faith of the apostle Paul, who in 2 Timothy 1:12 said, "I know whom I have believed, and I am convinced that he is able to guard until that Day what has been entrusted to me." It is the experience of the blind man, who, after recovering his sight through the power and mercy of Jesus, exclaimed, "One thing I do know, that though I was blind, now I see" (John 9:25).

When you have experience of how God through his Word changed your life, you can speak with a vibrant confidence and certainty about what he's done for you:

"My life was empty, but Jesus filled it."

"I was an addict, but Jesus set me free."

"I had no purpose or meaning, but now God has given me direction."

"My life was broken, but he put all the pieces back together."

The Christian faith is not an argument or a debate or a theological proposition. It is a declaration. We have a know-so salvation: "I write these things to you who believe in the name of the Son of God that you may *know* that you have eternal life" (1 John 5:13, emphasis added). In a time of so much confusion and misunderstanding and so many lies, the child of God can declare, "Blessed assurance, Jesus is mine."

And the best way to know God's Word in this deep, life-changing way is to spend time in it regularly. Daily. Keep coming back to it again and again, making this a habit in your life. Life will come into clearer focus as you read the Scripture, whether that's a single verse or a lengthy narrative. It is important not to rush. We're not just checking a box for daily Bible study but inviting God's Word to penetrate our minds and hearts, to transform the way we think and live. We're inviting the Holy Spirit to teach us and train us in godly living. Proverbs 1:23 says, "Behold, I will pour out my spirit to you; I will make my words known to you." This is a promise that comes straight out of the Word of God: Not only do we have his word, but we have his Spirit to make it known to us.

Getting Started

To have an effective time with God, start by keeping it simple. There's no wrong place to start—either at the beginning of the Old Testament or the beginning of the New Testament will work. All of it is effective because all of it is God's Word. With all the Bible study tools and technologies available today, we can sometimes miss the simplicity of just reading and reflecting on the Bible.

The important part is to make reading God's Word a habit in your life. Read it consistently, line by line, verse by verse, assimilating what you are reading. Read and then reread. There are more specific strategies we'll get to later in this chapter, but I want to begin by saying the important thing is to just get started.

One way I reread the Bible and keep it fresh is by using different translations. Sometimes I pick a different translation per year for reading through the Bible. It's possible to get bored reading the Bible, not because the Bible is boring but because we as people tend to let our minds wander when we're reading something that looks familiar. So mix it up, stay diligent, and discipline yourself into forming a habit of Bible reading and studying.

There are days when you'll miss your Bible reading. Don't beat yourself up about it, but instead start over the next day. You may be sick or traveling or frankly just too tired, or the kids have hijacked your day so that you missed your time in God's Word. When that happens, just push restart. Christian living is not a sprint but a marathon. Once you've formed the habit of Bible reading, you'll find a way to keep going because you know God is transforming your life. You're getting to know Jesus more and more, and he is speaking to your heart, leading you forward.

Finding the Right Bible for You

If you're a new Christian or young in your faith, one of the first steps to spending daily time in God's Word is finding the right Bible for you. It can be confusing trying to figure out which Bible to choose. After all, there are many translations and paraphrases of the Scriptures, multiple study Bibles, and other current versions of God's Word. The most notable are the King James Version, the New King James, the English Standard Version, the New American Standard Bible, the New International Version, and the New Living Translation. These are all worthwhile Bibles I would recommend, and I'd encourage you to choose one of them.

But which one? The best Bible for you is the one you will actually read! I would encourage you to talk to your pastor or a spiritual leader or mentor and get counsel, and then invest in a Bible you can make your own. Today there are also digital editions of most of the major translations. I'm grateful for these and use them often, but I'd recommend having a printed copy of God's Word always at hand, which you can carry with you wherever you go. It's easier for most people to navigate a Bible that is "old school"—one that's printed and bound.

A Brief History of Bible Translations

I'm grateful for the translations of the Bible and the translators who labored to create them. The Bible has been translated into all the major languages as well as many dialects around the world. One of my favorite spots on earth is the Museum of the Bible in Washington, D.C. In the museum is a section called Illuminations. This compelling room is a tribute to the translators and their translations of the Bible. As of today the Bible has been translated into 736 languages, but this number is growing rapidly. I praise God for this. Translating the Scripture is a great work, and the scholars who do this are contributing tremendously to the advancement of the Christian faith across the globe. Jesus told us to go into all the world and make disciples (Matthew 28:19). This presumes that the gospel and the message of the Bible would be available in the languages of all the nations, so translating the Bible is critical to fulfilling Jesus' Great Commission.

There was a time in history when most people had no copy of the Bible that they could read. In fact, many religious leaders actually prevented common people from owning a personal copy of the Bible. William Tyndale lived over four centuries ago, and in his era the church mandated that only its leaders could read and interpret the Bible. These religious elitists refused to allow the Bible to be translated from Latin to the language of the people, until God placed it on Tyndale's heart to give the people an opportunity to read the Word of God for themselves.

So Tyndale undertook the daunting and even dangerous work of translating the Bible into English. This devoted follower of Jesus worked night and day, month after month, for eleven years. He taught himself Hebrew so he could translate the Old Testament. His life was one of courageous faith, as he was threatened many times. But he persevered through the persecution till at last he had completed the New Testament in 1525. The Tyndale translation of the New Testament was printed and distributed across the English-speaking world. Sadly, before he could complete his English translation of the Old Testament, he was taken prisoner and executed. Ever faithful to God, this brave Christian stood on the gallows platform and prayed, "Lord, open the eyes of the king of England."

Tyndale died a martyr in 1536, but just a few years later, God answered the bold prayer of this righteous man when the king of England, Henry VIII, ruled that publishers were permitted to translate the Bible into English. In 1611, the authorized version of King James I of England was published. This is now known as the King James Version of the Bible, and it's still in use today. As a young man, Tyndale promised God that he would make it possible for every plowboy to have access to the Bible. His story is a testimony to the preservation of Scripture and the proclamation of God's Word to the ends of the earth.

Another notable benchmark in the history of the Bible is the Geneva Study Bible of 1557. This was the first version in English to include verse divisions. It also included biblical maps, tables, chapter summaries, and section titles. This helped readers to navigate their Bibles by finding chapters and verses. The Geneva Bible became the most used Bible in English by Protestant Christians, which would have included such Englishmen as William Shakespeare, John Bunyan, and the pilgrims.

I give you just a small piece of the history of Bible translations to remind you how God has guided his Word into the minds and hearts of people and guarded it through the generations. We should give thanks to our God for the students and scholars of the Bible who delivered his eternal

Word in the languages of various peoples. This includes modern translators and those who revise the numerous versions of the Bible that enable us to read, study, and understand God's Word.

One translator of the Bible who paraphrased the New Testament was J. B. Phillips. He testified that there was such power in the Bible that as he was doing the translation, it felt as if he were rewiring an old house with the electricity still on. In other words, the Word of God is nothing to be trifled with. We should always humbly keep in mind that the work of translation is the work of God by his Spirit through those who have devoted their lives to studying the original biblical languages of Hebrew, Greek, and Aramaic, and given us a text we Christians can trust as the Word of God. We are praying that the Bible will be translated into every tribal language dialect and people group on the planet, and according to Wycliffe Bible Translators, there are still 1,268 languages and dialects to go. Pray and invest your financial resources in getting the message of Christ and the Bible to every person and every nation and every tribe.

Your Mental Approach as You Read God's Word

In James 1:23–25, we're told that the Bible is like a mirror. There are several ways people can look into a mirror. You can look with curiosity like a man who sees himself, realizes he's a mess, but walks away and does nothing because he doesn't care how he looks. Sometimes we approach the Word of God in the same way. We come to church, take a brief look, and go home unchanged. We don't see deeply enough. We don't see ourselves as we really are. A mirror can be most revealing, it can be most convicting, but only if we focus on what we're seeing and let it change us.

I know people who are merely sermon tasters. They get all excited about discovering some theological prophetic passage or another. It's fine to be excited about the facts of the Bible, but your relationship to God's Word has to be more than that. You can't read the Bible and just say, "Isn't that interesting?" We should be more than just curious when it comes to God's Word.

Others approach the Bible, the mirror of God's Word, with cynicism. They love to put it under their critical eye. But remember this: The Bible is not on trial. It has passed the test of time. When you look into the Bible, *you* are the one on trial.

I remember when I saw the *Mona Lisa* in person, my one and only time. I could barely get a glimpse of the famous painting because the crowd was pressing in all around it, some even taking selfies with the old girl. When I was finally able to get a good look at it, frankly, I wasn't all that impressed. It was smaller than I'd expected and not as great as I'd hoped. But then someone reminded me that when you speak of the *Mona Lisa*, a work of art that has endured from generation to generation since 1506, the painting is not on trial. You are!

Likewise, we should look with carefulness at God's Word, remembering we are the ones being judged, not it. James 1:25 says, "But the one who looks into the perfect law, the law of liberty, and perseveres, being no hearer who forgets but a doer who acts, he will be blessed in his doing." In other words, we're to look intently. *Intently* is the same word that was used when Peter came to the empty tomb of Jesus and gazed into it. The word implies there's something important there to see.

James 1:21 says we are to receive the Word of God with meekness and openness. This means we're to welcome the Word. Do you welcome the Word? A carnal Christian—in other words, an immature Christian—has no appetite for God's Word. They let it pass over them rather than let it fill them up. Verse 19 says we must be quick to hear, which means we should always be ready for the Word of God to speak to us. When you go to church and listen to your pastor preach, you should be just as prepared to listen as the pastor is prepared to preach.

Jesus often said, "Be careful how you hear." This doesn't apply to literal hearing only, such as when the Word is preached; it's also about how we take in God's Word when we read it ourselves. The Bible says, "Be still, and know that I am God" (Psalm 46:10).

Being still means we should be quick to hear and slow to speak. Sometimes we can't hear because we're always talking, but God gave us one mouth and two ears—we ought to listen twice as much as we speak. We ought to be like Samuel when we come to God's Word and pray, saying, "Speak, [Lord,] for your servant hears" (1 Samuel 3:10), rather than "Listen, Lord, for your servant speaks."

Mirrors can reveal, but God's mirror, the Bible, can also restore. The ministry of the Word, when you welcome its truth into your life, will transform you by the Spirit of God. Your very countenance changes when Christ lives in you, and the Word of God dwells in you richly. As a child of God looks into the Word of God, he sees the Son of God and is transformed by the Spirit of God to demonstrate the glory of God. The ministry of the mirror of God's Word is there to make you look and act like Jesus. We're transformed by the renewing of our minds and by the truth. Do people see Jesus in you because you have seen Jesus in God's Word?

A Practical Approach to Bible Study

In the *Life Application Study Bible*, there's an application pyramid given by senior editor Dave Veerman, who suggests that readers ask nine questions of any biblical text.

1. People: Who are the people, and how are they like us today?

2. Place: What is the setting, and what are the similarities to our world?

3. Plot: Is there any conflict or tension? How would I have reacted in that situation?

4. Point: What was the intended message for the people to hear? What did God want them to learn, feel, or do?

5. Principles: What are the timeless truths?

6. Present: How's this relevant in our world today?

7. Parallels: Where does this truth apply to my life at home, at work or at school, in church, or in my neighborhood?

8. Personal: What attitude, action, value, or belief needs to change in me?

9. Plan: What should be my first steps in taking action?

This is one of many step-by-step tools that can help you dive deeper into God's Word. But the important thing is to look at God's Word carefully and then let it change you. Notice that this method starts by focusing on the specific details—the who, what, when, and where—and then moves on to bigger themes. What is this passage trying to say? What does it tell me about God? What does it tell me about myself? What is it telling me about the world or the culture I live in?

Lastly, whether you're using this method or not, the focus should shift to life change. How should this passage of Scripture affect what I do or think or say? How can God use it to make me more like Christ? That's what James was saying about our looking in the mirror. Don't just look at it with amused curiosity, but instead be ready to obey what God is asking you to do.

Sharing God's Word with Others

The challenge for believers is to live Christlike lives in this present world, which is described in Philippians 2:15. We live in a crooked and perverse generation, warped and diseased, twisted and foolish. As Christians we are to be different. In fact, we *must* be different to make a difference, and the way to do this is to hold fast to the word of life (Philippians 2:16).

To hold fast to God's Word also means offering it to others, as the "word of life" is the answer to the problems of the world today. We offer it to others because we have received this life. I've recently gone through my library and discarded many of the books I've collected from the past because in many ways, these are lifeless books. They're books that no longer have a purpose. But the Bible contains life, and if we care about others, we should want to share this with them.

In Acts 5, we read of the apostles and their witness of the gospel. An angel of the Lord appeared to them and said, "Go and stand in the temple and speak to the people all the words of this Life" (Acts 5:19–20). That's why we share God's Word: to bring life to others. And 1 Peter 1:23 says, "Since you have been born again, not of perishable seed but of imperishable, through the living and abiding word of God . . ." We are born again by receiving Jesus Christ and trusting in the message of God's Word, the gospel. The Spirit of God takes the Word of God and imparts the Son of God into our very hearts. He who has the Son has life, and he who has not the Son does not have life. One of the most important verses in the Bible is John 5:24, where Jesus said, "Truly, truly, I say to you, whoever hears my word and believes him who sent me has eternal life. He does not come into judgment, but has passed from death to life." Hebrews 4:12 adds, "For the word of God is living and active. . . ." Since the Bible has life in it, it cannot be destroyed, and it is always relevant to the needs of every stage and age of history.

When Jesus raised the dead, as in the case of Lazarus, he spoke and the dead man came alive. In the same way, when

God speaks today, the dead come alive. Every salvation story is a miracle. It is the story of God's grace and power to save us from our sin, and to give us a brand-new life.

When I was a pastor in a little town in Oklahoma named Holbert, I became good friends with one of our members, Dr. Van Howard. One day I was called to the hospital for an emergency with one of our young women who was facing an all-day battle for not only the life of her unborn child, but for her own life. At the end of the day, the mother delivered the child with the able help of Dr. Howard. I remember sitting in the small hospital cafeteria late that night and saying to my doctor friend, "Doc, that birth was a miracle," to which he replied, "Preacher, every birth is a miracle." He was right, and every new birth is a miracle too because the Word of God brings life.

The Bible also sustains life. When you receive eternal life, this life must be nurtured and nourished. You have an inner person that needs care, for your soul needs spiritual clothing, bathing, exercise, and nourishment. How do you feed the inner person? You are what you think, and so you feed yourself emotionally, intellectually, and spiritually on the Word of God. We need spiritual milk and should desire the sincere milk of the Word. We need bread, but "man shall not live by bread alone, but by every word that comes from the mouth of God" (Matthew 4:4). We also need sweetness in our food, and God's Word, according to Psalm 119:103, is sweet: "How sweet are your words to my taste, sweeter than honey to my mouth!" God's Word is called honey and bread nine times in Psalm 119.

We are refreshed and renewed and revived by reading God's Word. I believe the Word of God can bring dead churches back to life, and dull Christians to a brand-new and exciting life. There's an old hymn by Philip P. Bliss that says, "Sing them over again to me, wonderful words of life; let me more of their beauty see, wonderful words of life."

Consistency in Reading God's Word

In Acts 17, we're told that the Berean believers searched the Scriptures daily. If you want to grow in your faith, you must nourish it, digesting the Word of God. The Word of God brings such joy to our lives, so study it regularly. And then store God's Word by absorbing it into your life, saturating your soul with the words of Scripture. Know it and then sow it by sharing the Word of God, holding fast to the word of life.

We are to delight in God's Word. I'm concerned about those who have no appetite for the Bible. Job said, "I have not departed from the commandment of his lips; I have treasured the words of his mouth more than my portion of food" (Job 23:12). When you love the Lord, you will have an insatiable appetite to know what he says. When you become a follower of Jesus, you should want to spend time with him. The Christian life is a daily walk with Christ. Like any relationship, it takes time to develop the bonds of friendship, and spending time with the Lord each day is essential and beyond just being a duty; it is a sacred privilege, a holy habit.

The most important appointment we make each day is our appointment to meet with Jesus, and the most successful people I know have a morning routine. In fact, the first part of our day determines the effectiveness of the rest of the day, such as whether we'll accomplish God's plans for us and be a blessing to others. This is why I choose to begin each day spending time with God and his Word. Whether you call it a quiet time, daily devotions, a morning watch, or a divine appointment, it is the way we meet with the Lord and grow in our relationship with him.

You may have a lot going on each day, but I assure you, your time with God is the most important time you will spend. I start virtually every day of my life with God's Word, which prepares me for my daily responsibilities and opportunities and sets my mind on what's really important. But more important, it helps me get my will aligned with the will of God. Jesus said in Matthew 6:33, "But seek first the kingdom of God and his righteousness, and all these things will be added to you."

So, as a matter of priority, I carve out Bible reading and prayer intentionally, so that I may pursue God, develop my faith, and strengthen and deepen my relationship with him. I love the way the prophet Isaiah says it: "In the morning my spirit longs for you . . . Be our strength every morning . . . The Sovereign LORD has given me a well-instructed tongue, to know the word that sustains the weary. He wakens me morning by morning, wakens my ear to listen like one being instructed" (Isaiah 26:9; 33:2; 50:4 NIV).

Our schedules are not all the same, and the timing of your appointment with God is flexible, but your commitment to spend time with him is not. You may need to get creative in carving out time for your daily devotions, but it is so very important that you make your spiritual development the first priority of your life. When we discipline ourselves in this, we are promised a blessing. "Blessed is the one who listens to me, watching daily at my gates, waiting beside my doors" (Proverbs 8:34).

Many people discipline themselves to exercise regularly. This is a good habit I certainly would recommend. But the question is, are you exercising your soul? The Bible says in 1 Timothy 4:8, "For while bodily training is of some value, godliness is of value in every way, as it holds promise for the present life and also for the life to come." If you want to grow stronger in your walk with Jesus, then realize faith is like a muscle that must be strengthened, and the way to spiritual vitality is by getting repetitions in God's Word on a daily basis.

The Bible Engagement Challenge

In an effort to see the impact of Bible reading, a radio program called *Back to the Bible* had 400,000 people surveyed. Their findings were astonishing. For those people who read the Bible three times or less a week, the life changes were minimal. Everything changes, however, when someone reads God's Word four or more times a week. As soon as God's Word became a part of the majority of someone's days, the effects were phenomenal. They were 57 percent less likely to get drunk, 68 percent less likely to participate in sex outside of marriage, 30 percent less likely to struggle with loneliness, 61 percent less likely to engage with pornography, 74 percent less likely to gamble, and 57 percent less likely to engage with all of these habits together. On the positive side, the report found that consistent Bible readers are 228 percent more likely to share their faith, 231 percent more likely to disciple others, and 407 percent more likely to memorize Scripture.[1]

Other spiritual disciplines were considered (prayer at least once a day and monthly attendance at a church), but it was made clear by the findings of the study that no single discipline was as effective in helping Christians combat the temptations listed above as regular reading of the Scriptures. The behavioral differences made by consistent, weekly Bible engagement were unparalleled.

This is not new knowledge for faithful Bible readers, as their lives and the Scriptures themselves attest to this truth. However, this article does illustrate and validate the words of Psalm 119:11: "I have stored up your word in my heart, that I might not sin against you."

You can start reading the Bible four or more times a week for yourself and see it change your life from the inside out. God's Word is alive and truly changes lives. It helps us live to please God and not ourselves, as God's Word is the only book you read that also reads you. In fact, God's Word is the only book where you can meet with the author, the Holy Spirit, as you read, so he can answer your questions!

Final Thoughts on Spending Time in God's Word

There are many portraits of the Word of God found in the Bible, and in each one we get a fresh glimpse of its power and effectiveness. Like word pictures, the Bible describes itself in ways easy for us to understand and appreciate.

First, the Word of God is a seed: "Since you have been born again, not of perishable seed but of imperishable, through the living and abiding word of God . . . the word of the Lord remains forever" (1 Peter 1:23, 25).

Second, the Word of God is a mirror: "But be doers of the word, and not hearers only, deceiving yourselves. For if anyone is a hearer of the word and not a doer, he is like a man who looks intently at his natural face in a mirror. For he looks at himself and goes away and at once forgets what he was like" (James 1:22–24).

Third, the Word of God is a sword: "And take the helmet of salvation, and the sword of the Spirit, which is the word of God" (Ephesians 6:17). "For the word of God is living and active, sharper than any two-edged sword, piercing to the division of soul and of spirit, of joints and of marrow, and discerning the thoughts and intentions of the heart" (Hebrews 4:12).

Fourth, the Word of God is a hammer: "Is not my word like fire, declares the LORD, and like a hammer that breaks the rock in pieces?" (Jeremiah 23:29).

Fifth, the Word of God is a lamp: "Your word is a lamp to my feet and a light to my path" (Psalm 119:105). "And we have something more sure, the prophetic word, to which you will do well to pay attention as to a lamp shining in a dark place, until the day dawns and the morning star rises in your hearts" (2 Peter 1:19).

Sixth, the Word of God is milk: "Like newborn infants, long for the pure spiritual milk, that by it you may grow up into salvation" (1 Peter 2:2).

Seventh, the Word of God is meat or solid food: "For though by this time you ought to be teachers, you need someone to teach you again the basic principles of the oracles of God. You need milk, not solid food, for everyone who lives on milk is unskilled in the word of righteousness, since he is a child. But solid food is for the mature, for those who have their powers of discernment trained by constant practice to distinguish good from evil" (Hebrews 5:12–14).

Eighth and last, the Word of God is a fire: "If I say, 'I will not mention him, or speak any more in his name,' there is in my heart as it were a burning fire shut up in my bones, and I am weary with holding it in, and I cannot" (Jeremiah 20:9). "They said to each other, 'Did not our hearts burn within us while he talked to us on the road, while he opened to us the Scriptures?'" (Luke 24:32).

One of the greatest organizations committed to promoting Bible reading throughout our society is The Gideons International. In 1985, they produced the following statement concerning the Word of God: "The Bible contains the mind of God, the state of man, the way of salvation, the doom of sinners, and the happiness of believers. Its doctrines are holy, its precepts are binding, its histories are true, and its decisions are immutable. Read it to be wise, believe it to be saved, and practice it to be holy. The Bible is the life book. In it we find the authority, authenticity, and accuracy of God's very word."

7  Knowing God's Will through Bible Reading

Success in life is knowing and doing the will of God, and if you want to be successful, truly successful, then you must understand the progressive realization of God's will for your life. But the question is, how can we know and do God's will? It is the question I suppose I've been asked more than any other in my many years as a pastor.

When it comes to knowing and doing God's will, start with the Bible. The Word of God is the will of God, and if you want to know what God is leading you to do, open his Word and open your heart to listen. Some Christians claim that God never says anything to them, and yet they rarely open their Bibles. Thankfully, God's Word tells us how we can discern and discover God's will. He makes his will clear in his Word because he wants you to know it.

The systematic study of the Scriptures will lead you to where only God can take you.

God's Clear Rules

How can we know God's will? Let's start with precepts. A precept is a rule that regulates behavior. God has spoken clearly on matters of moral choice, the ethical decisions we make and how we live our lives. He has given us commandments, which are to be kept. These are the moral standards and guidelines for many of the decisions we must make on a daily basis: Do not steal, do not bear false witness, do not covet, do not commit adultery, and so on.

God's will always aligns with his Word. If we commit to always obeying God's Word, we'll find ourselves walking in the will of God. I once heard the great preacher Stephen Olford say, "God will not take us one step further than the measure of our obedience to him." This is true.

What does God's Word say about God's will specifically? What are his precepts for us? For one, it is God's will that we live godly lives. For example, 1 Thessalonians 4:3 states, "For this is the will of God, your sanctification: that you abstain from sexual immorality." Being sanctified means that we are becoming more like Christ every day, maturing as Christians. The Spirit of God enables us to be more and more like him, to have the mind of Jesus in the way we live and love others. This is his will for us.

It is also God's will that we live grateful lives: 1 Thessalonians 5:18 says, "Give thanks in all circumstances; for this is the will of God in Christ Jesus for you." And it is God's will that we live humble, merciful, and just lives: "He has told you, O man, what is good; and what does the LORD require of you but to do justice, and to love kindness, and to walk humbly with your God?" (Micah 6:8).

The Bible is filled with such precepts, but when Jesus was asked which among them is the most important commandment, he said, "You shall love the Lord your God with all your heart and with all your soul and with all your mind. This is the great and first commandment. And a second is like it: You shall love your neighbor as yourself. On these two commandments depend all the Law and the Prophets" (Matthew 22:37–40). Does this mean that if we try our best to do these two things, we can ignore the rest of the Bible? Certainly not. All of God's Word matters and is a guide to help us better love God and love others. And if we think we can figure these things out on our own, we are mistaken.

God's Will and Prayer

Another way we can discern and then do the will of God is by prayer. Knowing God's will is a result of prayer, which we can see by the way Jesus taught us to pray: "Your kingdom come, *your will be done*, on earth as it is in heaven" (Matthew 6:10, emphasis added). Jesus offers us the perfect example of a life of prayer that seeks God's will, as demonstrated in the Garden of Gethsemane when he prayed "not my will but your will be done." God speaks to us and leads us when we pray. In fact, the Lord said, "Ask, and it will be given to you; seek, and you will find; knock, and it will be opened to you" (Matthew 7:7).

I'm often asked to help people discover God's will for their lives, and I'm always happy to give counsel—it is good to seek godly counsel. But sometimes, when I ask them if they've prayed about it, the answer is, "Sort of, but not really." This makes me wonder, Why ask me for guidance when you haven't yet asked God? God will give us guidance when we ask him. Remember, prayer is not just talking to God; it's also listening to God. Prayer is two-way communication.

So how do we approach God in prayer? First, we speak with words of praise and adoration. We worship first, and then we ask for what we need. After that we listen to God speak.

As a child, my grandpa taught me the story of Samuel as we read the Scripture together. This story fascinated me then and still does to this day. Samuel served as an apprentice to a prophet, an older man named Eli. The older man treated the younger man as a son, so when Samuel was awakened by a voice, he thought it was Eli calling for him. He promptly got up and asked, "What do you need?" After this had happened three times, the older man of God told him that the next time, instead of coming to him, he should simply pray, "Speak, Lord, your servant is listening." Samuel went back and prayed this short but powerful prayer: "Lord, speak to me. I'm listening."

This was a long time ago, of course, but I believe God still speaks similarly today. When we ask him, he will speak to us. I have prayed many times, "Lord, show me your will." Samuel's short supplication indicates a strong desire to know and do God's will, which is what all of us should want. Psalm 37:4 says that we are to delight ourselves in the Lord, and he will give us the desires of our hearts. When we pray and seek God, when we desire and delight in him, he will put in our hearts the desires and the prayers that will help us discern God's will. God speaks to us when we have a desire to please him and a heart to obey him.

While prayer is distinct from reading God's Word, you'll find they are closely related and aligned. When Samuel went back to his room, he then expected God to speak. When you go to church to worship God, listen to your pastor preach God's Word. Do you go expectantly, praying that the Spirit of God would speak to you through the Word of God through the servant of God? Do you listen prayerfully and willingly to not only know but to *do* what God says? David prayed, "Let me hear what God the LORD will speak, for he will speak peace to his people, to his saints . . ." (Psalm 85:8). If you truly want to hear God's voice and fulfill his will for your life, you will not be disappointed. If you want God to speak to you, he will when you get alone with him. Wait for him. Expect for him to hear you when you pray "Speak, Lord, for your servant is listening."

Humbly Listening to the Lord

One other thing to keep in mind about Samuel is that when this young prophet-in-the-making prayed, he spoke to the Lord in humility. He described himself as God's servant, which demonstrated his submission and revealed a childlike faith that was tender and trusting. Of course, he was literally a child at the time, but we can adopt this same posture or attitude whenever we approach the Lord. When we pray, "Lord, I surrender my will to do your will," we will begin to hear him speak. "Lord, your will, anywhere, anytime, at any cost" is a prayer I learned as a young Christian, which has served me well over the years.

There's a woman in the New Testament named Mary, and each time we meet her, she's at a significant and strategic place: at the feet of Jesus. That's where she listened to him teach (Luke 10:39). Sit quietly before the Lord and let him teach you his way and his will. God's will is for you to live under the authority of his lordship. It is to show up each day and, in effect, report for duty as we surrender to serve him. In knowing and doing God's will, we submit ourselves to his sovereignty. In Romans 12:1–2, the Scripture says we are to present our bodies as living sacrifices, holy and acceptable to God, so that we can discern what is the will of God, what is good and acceptable and perfect. As you seek the Lord and give yourself unconditionally to him, you will discover his will right in front of you. God will speak to you and reveal to you his will.

In Acts 13:2, we're told that as the believers in the church at Antioch were worshiping the Lord and fasting, the Holy Spirit said, "Set apart for me Barnabas and Saul for the work to which I have called them." These men became the first missionaries sent by a church in the New Testament. How did the Holy Spirit speak? Not audibly, but personally, spiritually, deeply within. They were moved and motivated to do God's will from within as they prayed, and God spoke to their hearts.

One of the biggest moments of my life came in the mid-1990s. I had been pastor of Prestonwood Church for three years, and it was apparent that the church was growing and needed to expand. We made every effort to expand at the location where the church was founded in Far North

Dallas, but it was becoming increasingly difficult to find the space required for the growing congregation. We had all kinds of building plans drawn up, with architects designing everything from sky bridges to parking garages. The church was willing to do whatever it took to continue growing and reaching people for Christ.

Around this time, I took my family on vacation to Colorado. On the first day of the trip, I went out for a run. While exercising, God spoke to me as clear as could be: *Jack, you're limiting what I want to do with Prestonwood.* I couldn't have imagined anything louder than that, even though it wasn't out loud but deep within my soul. That was it. Instantly I knew what God meant. His plans for our church were bigger and better than what we were planning.

I knew in my heart what God wanted our church to do, which was to seek his will as to how we could expand. I gathered together the church leaders, and we began to pray and seek God's will. Through that process, God led us to relocating the church, moving our entire congregation of over 12,000 members to a new site. We didn't know where exactly, but we did know God was leading us. It was during that run when God spoke to me that the massive expansion of Prestonwood began to take shape.

Of course, God doesn't speak to just pastors and religious leaders; God will speak to all believers who are willing to listen to him and obey him. God will grant us the wisdom to make sound decisions according to his will. James 1:5 gives us a great and unrestricted promise: "If any of you lacks wisdom, let him ask God, who gives generously to all without reproach, and it will be given him." God invites us to ask him for wisdom from above. Wisdom simply means to see things from God's perspective. According to Ephesians 5:17, wisdom is to "understand what the will of the Lord is."

Wisdom, then, is synonymous with understanding, and clearly God has promised us his wisdom. Wisdom has been called "sanctified common sense" because God has given his children minds to think and reason, and Christians have the mind of Christ. So don't be afraid to put his wisdom to good use. The Presbyterian pastor Donald Barnhouse once said that "ninety-nine percent of the will of God is above the neck." When we pray, God speaks, and when he does, we are to simply respond, "Yes, Lord, your servant is listening."

God Reveals His Will by Providing a Way

God not only speaks to us through precepts and through prayer, but through providence. Providence means to see in advance: *pro* meaning "before" and *video* meaning "to see." God works purposefully and providentially in our lives through our circumstances and the choices we make. He opens and closes doors in ways that sometimes we understand and sometimes we don't. In Revelation 3:8, God says, "Behold, I have set before you an open door, which no one is able to shut." God's unseen hand of providence is working relentlessly, constructively, and creatively in the Christian's life.

I've seen this in my life many times. As a high school student, one of my ambitions was to play baseball, if not at the professional level, then at the college level. I worked hard, played hard, and developed my skills, praying that somehow, someday I could play Division 1 baseball. I even prayed it would be in the American Southwest Conference, which is one of the highest levels of college baseball in Texas and in the nation.

After a successful season my junior year, Baylor University's head coach, "Dutch" Schroeder, invited me to come to Baylor and play. Prayers answered. They offered me a scholarship, which was important because I doubted whether my parents could have afforded for me to attend Baylor. After a visit to the university in Waco, Texas, I agreed to the offer. Everything was coming together beautifully. I was headed to a well-known and respected Baptist university, where I could prepare myself for ministry while also playing baseball. Bible study and baseball—for me, it couldn't get much better than that.

After another successful season of playing ball my senior year, I was ready to pack my bags and glove and go to Baylor. The only problem was that I hadn't heard from Coach Schroeder. He had assured me we would sign the papers after my senior year in high school. It was now the beginning of summer, 1968. I was graduating, but still waiting and wondering what was happening with Baylor and Coach Schroeder.

Somehow, my pastor, Fred Swank, heard about my situation and connected me to his alma mater, Hardin-Simmons University. I was offered a spot on their team and committed to them, even though it felt like Plan B. The next day, something truly amazing happened. I received a letter from Coach Schroeder, inviting me to come and play baseball at Baylor, but the letter had been delayed due to the illness of his daughter. He suggested that we get together and make it official.

I had a big decision to make. Should I back out on Hardin-Simmons, the university I'd already committed to, after having told the coach and my pastor and my parents that I was following God's will in attending a smaller school and program? Or should I keep my earlier promise and head to West Texas? I prayed about it and asked God to lead me. I turned to a Bible promise, which was on the wall of my room in East Fort Worth, Texas—found in Proverbs 3:5–6: "Trust in the LORD with all your heart, and do not lean on your own understanding. In all your ways acknowledge him, and he will make straight your paths." It appeared that God had closed one door and opened another, but now two doors stood open.

I believed that God had led me on a path that was different from what I'd expected. By faith I also believed that his plans were better than mine, so I decided to keep my commitment to do God's will anywhere, anytime, and attended Hardin-Simmons University, where I studied for the ministry and played four years of college baseball. Looking back, I see the providence of God in that decision. He showed me which door to walk through. As a college athlete I began speaking and preaching throughout West Texas, and I was given many opportunities to hone my preaching skills during those years. I studied the Bible under the tutelage of wonderful professors, who loved me personally and taught me God's Word. And I met a beautiful freshman girl from Mineral Wells, Texas, by the name of Deb, who had my heart the moment she said hello. After a brief romance, within the year we were married as college sweethearts.

We've now been married for fifty-four years, and God has given us three wonderful children, along with their spouses, and eight grandchildren. The Great Eight. The Lord has given Deb and me a life that we could have never imagined, serving him together. I've often wondered, What if I had missed God's will in those formative years of my life? What if I'd chosen to take a different path outside of God's will? I know that when God doesn't rule, he over-rules, but I also know that God had a perfect path for me. And everything in my life would have been different had I chosen a different direction that was my way instead of God's way. I would have had a different life and a different wife, different children and grandchildren, and my preparation for ministry and my relationship with my home pastor all would have dramatically changed. This is God's providence.

In Proverbs 19:21, God says that when we sincerely seek to do what he wants of us, his purpose will stand. His will and ways are always best. It may be a different road than we had planned, but God is good. "For those who love God all things work together for good . . ." (Romans 8:28). Trust in the Lord. Don't depend on your own understanding. Put him first in all that you do, and he will direct your paths (Proverbs 3:5–6). I also love Psalm 37:23–24, which says, "The steps of a man are established by the LORD, when he delights in his way; though he fall, he shall not be cast headlong, for the LORD upholds his hand."

113

God Makes a Way

I've discovered in the providence of God that what God originates, he orchestrates. He makes a way. When it says that God clears the way in Proverbs 3:6, the Hebrew word *yashar* is used, which means "God will clear the path." He will make a way can also be translated as he will make your paths straight.

I'm a big fan of football, and one of the most important things that happens in a football game is when the offensive line blocks for the running back. For winning teams, it all starts up front with the offensive line. When the offensive line is effective, the running back reads his blockers and then races at full speed through the hole they created. Similarly, the Lord opens and clears the path in all that we do. And all we need to do is look for the hole or opening, then follow where God is leading.

There's an old song I used to sing as a child: "My Lord knows the way through the wilderness. All I have to do is follow." When we obey God and commit to doing his will, he will open a hole so wide that you'll be surprised by how easy it is to run through. I'm not saying there aren't difficult times in which we must do difficult things in doing God's will; I'm saying God will always clear the path for us. David Wilkerson was quoted by my friend Tim Dilena as saying, "God always makes a way for a praying man [or woman]."

Athletes talk about being "in the flow." This is a condition described as being in a state mentally whereby things come easier. When athletes are in the flow, they move easily forward, and when we get in the flow of God's Spirit as we live in his Word, God will remove the obstacles in front of us so that we can go forward. When you obey the Word and walk in the flow of God's Spirit, you'll find that you can easily follow and fulfill God's good and perfect and acceptable will for your life.

You will discover that the path he chose for you is what you would have chosen for yourself had you known all the facts. Trust him always, and he will take you to places you could never have imagined. At the end of Paul's prayer in Ephesians 3:20, he adds, "To him who is able to do far more abundantly than all that we ask or think, according to the power at work within us . . ."

God leads us by his providence, and he leads us with peace. When we live by his Word and do his perfect will, we will experience a sense of abiding, assuring peace, a deep confidence that is consistent and continual. According to Galatians 5, one of the fruits of the Spirit is peace, and when we are walking in the Spirit, we can expect a supernatural sense of well-being. God's plans and purposes come with his peace. Philippians 4:6–7 tells us, "Do not be anxious about anything, but in everything by prayer and supplication with thanksgiving let your requests be made known to God. And the peace of God, which surpasses all understanding, will guard your hearts and your minds in Christ Jesus."

God's peace gives us a security and a serenity of mind that is unexplainable, beyond our ability to comprehend. This peace is promised when we occupy our minds with what is true, honorable, just, pure, lovely, and commendable (Philippians 4:8). We are to meditate on these things and then do them. "What you have learned and received and heard and seen in me—practice these things, and the God of peace will be with you" (Philippians 4:9).

God Leads through His People

God also leads us through his people. Paul said in the same passage, Philippians 4, that what you have seen in me, put to practice, when seeking God's will. In other words, seek out godly counsel and Christlike examples. Invite those people into your life who can give you prayerful counsel and help confirm God's best for you.

You can start by going to your church and listening to God's servant in the pulpit. Open God's Word and ask him by his Spirit to speak to you. Go to a church where the Bible is taught faithfully, where Jesus is exalted. Go with a Bible in your hand, ready to hear the Word from whoever is preaching and teaching. Find a spiritual mentor who can advance you forward in the will of God. Listen to a podcast of biblical teaching or a sermon broadcast on radio, television, or the internet. Some of the greatest teachers in the world are available through such channels; just make sure you're hearing the Bible and not human opinions. Look for solid biblical teachers and expositors of God's Word, people who magnify Christ and his gospel. God places people in our lives to instruct us and help us go forward in his will.

If you're a young person and God has given you wise Christian parents who know and love God, talk things over with them. Listen to the people God has put in your life to guide you. And if it's not already obvious who those people are, then seek out someone of integrity who can offer wise counsel. Most devoted Christians would be happy to speak with you and answer any questions you may have.

But whatever your age or season of life, there are people God has provided who can help confirm what God wants you to do. Such people have walked where you want to go, trusted God to accomplish his will, overcome adversity, pursued God's will, and persevered through tough times. They are great examples for you to follow.

Find other Christians in your church who will encourage you and equip you as you walk with God. Join a small-group Bible study and grow in the faith with your fellow believers. We need the fellowship of the Church; we cannot live independently from the body of Christ and expect to make wise decisions.

So there it is. When you fill your mind with God's truth and think like him, you will walk right into his will with confidence that you're doing the right thing. In other words, think right and you will do right, and as a result you'll live with a radical calmness in your spirit. There is no fear or anxiety in the center of God's will. Just perfect peace. In fact, the safest and happiest place on earth is in the will of God. The Hebrew word for peace is *shalom*, which means well-being. Isaiah 26:3 speaks of this peace: "You keep him in perfect peace whose mind is stayed on you, because he trusts in you." When we read, remember, and rehearse Scripture, our thinking and way of living are transformed as God's plans become our plans.

Always keep in mind, God's Word is God's will. The Bible is a book to be learned and then lived in obedience to his will, which in turn will bring peace, joy, and purpose to your life. Jesus said, "Seek first the kingdom of God and his righteousness, and all these things will be added to you. Therefore do not be anxious about tomorrow . . ." (Matthew 6:33–34). Approach each day with the enthusiasm that comes by realizing God's Spirit lives in you, and you are in his will because his Word is alive in you.

8 Protecting Yourself from Bad Bible Reading

In Harper Lee's 1960 novel *To Kill a Mockingbird*, her character Miss Maudie says, "Sometimes the Bible in the hand of one man is worse than a whiskey bottle in the hand of [another]." How true that is! Most Christians know enough about the Bible to be dangerous. Sales of the Bible in America is a massive industry ($2.5 billion annually), yet it is the bestseller few read and even fewer understand.

The Bible can be a moving target. One can strip it down, twist it, misread it, add to it, supplement it, and even overrule it, and unfortunately, 95 percent of the average congregation will not realize it. Why? Because many Americans no longer *know* the Bible. The evidence is overpowering that contemporary Christianity is Bible-*ish* at best, and in some cases, Bible-*less*. The American Bible Society releases an annual *State of the Bible* report, and their research is persuasive that the influence of the Bible in America is in decline. Everyone has an opinion about the Bible. Politicians attempt to use it, Grammy Award winners quote it, and Hollywood has portrayed it on the big screen. Yet most are oblivious to the Bible's basic content, meaning, and message.

The Bible is not held in the esteem it once was, as over the last 150 years, America has drifted from its biblical focus. It's remarkable to recall that even though Abraham Lincoln wasn't a member of any church, the Bible was so valued as an authority that he quoted from it four strategic times in his second inaugural address on March 4, 1865. President Lincoln used words ascribed to Jesus in Matthew 18:7 and, using the Bible, pronounced God's judgment on our nation for the moral bankruptcy of slavery.

The unwillingness of many Americans to dig deeper into the Scriptures is not related to a lack of options. The Gideons give away a Bible every second. One publisher sells more than sixty different editions of the Bible. Clearly, the challenge of biblical illiteracy in America is not because of a shortage of Bibles, but rather knowledge and appreciation of the Bible's message.

The Bible is a diverse love story. Actually, it is the greatest break-up-and-get-back-together story the world has ever known. The message of the Bible is that even though we are not what we should be, God loves us, wants to redeem us, and has a purpose for our lives. The plotline of the Bible is like a sweeping romance. The characters fall in love (God's love for us), they break up (the Fall), and then they get back together (Jesus and redemption). Once a person encounters the story of the Bible's history and preservation and the cost that was involved—*and it was a terrible cost*—one can never again open the Scriptures with the same detached, careless attitude.

The story of how the Bible has come to us is a tale of heroism, courage, persecution, betrayal, and towering faith in a God who raises the dead, mixed through the centuries with the blood of martyrs. If 80 percent of Americans believe the Bible is God's Word, shouldn't we show the Bible some respect by knowing more about it? The goal of this chapter is to reinforce better Bible-reading skills and then offer resources, vital methods, and practical tools all Bible readers need not only to avoid bad Bible reading, but to bring them closer to the Lord by embracing his message to them through his Word.

It Starts with a Deep Reverence for God's Message

"The works of his hands are faithful and just; all his precepts are trustworthy; they are established forever and ever, to be performed with faithfulness and uprightness. He sent redemption to his people; he has commanded his covenant forever. Holy and awesome is his name!" (Psalm 111:7–9). The psalmist originally wrote these words to be sung in worship to God. In its original Hebrew form, it is an alphabetical acrostic containing twenty-two lines, and each line begins with the next successive Hebrew letter. With its focus on God's works, it's like saying that from A to Z, all of God's deeds call for praise.

In verses 7–9, the psalmist zeroes in on the works of God as seen in his truth, justice, instruction, and redemption. We know of these things because he has revealed them through Scripture, the divinely inspired Word of God, and that Word is trustworthy! The psalmist's statement, "all his precepts are trustworthy," is a confession of trust and respect for God's Word and its application to his life.

This passage reflects a "divine agreement." The psalmist acknowledged both the covenant and the redemption established by God, but it was more than a mental acknowledgement. The psalmist wrote with absolute faith in the works and words of God. We also live in divine agreement when we are one with God and seeing his world through the eyes of faith. We choose to see things from God's perspective. We can entrust the difficult decisions in our lives to God because his Word—his instructions to us—is trustworthy.

The Word of God stands forever, and it empowers our walk with Christ. Therefore, it is not enough to know the Bible intellectually; in fact, we don't really know the Bible until we encounter it experientially. We learn God's truth as we apply it to our lives. To that end, I encourage you to adopt these principles:

- **The K-D Principle:** *Know* what the Word says, then *Do* what the Word says.
- **The M-A Principle:** Discover the *Meaning* of the Scripture, then *Apply* that meaning to your life. Only when you understand the meaning of Scripture can you have the confidence to apply that meaning to your life.

It is not enough to *know* about God's redemption; we must *experience* it for ourselves! God's Word is clear: We can never come into a right relationship with God on our own (Romans 3:10–12). Thankfully, God has "sent redemption to his people" through his Son, Jesus Christ (Psalm 111:9). The Scriptures, God's trustworthy instructions, point us to Jesus, our Redeemer. Only God can redeem us, for he has paid the price to set us free.

It gets even better! The redemption God lavishes on his people cannot fail but is confirmed by his covenant—a covenant he's ordained to live on forever. Moses connected this covenant with God's love, or more specifically, with his gracious covenant loyalty (Deuteronomy 7:9). God's love remains faithful even when we are unfaithful; his covenant of love cannot fail. He welcomes us into his family in a covenant to protect us, provide for us, and commune with us. This covenant is not based on our performance, but on his redemption accomplished in Jesus Christ.

The psalmist's response to the redemption and covenant was worship: "Holy and awesome is his name!" The universe around us reveals a God who is both awe-inspiring and holy, set apart from his creation. Scripture reveals the salvation and covenant of God, aspects of his nature and character that are equally holy and awe-inspiring. Like the psalmist, we should be drawn to worship him who loves us so, and that means treating God's Word with the reverence it deserves.

The C.I.A. Bible Study Method

At Prestonwood Baptist Church, our apologetics and cultural engagement pastor, Dr. Jeremiah Johnston, teaches the C.I.A. Bible study method in the church's LifeGroup Bible Study classes. Jeremiah gave me permission to share some of it here because many have found this method extremely helpful as "best practices" in Bible reading.

It's not hard to believe in heresy or to become a heretic. All a person needs is the Bible and no context and/or Jesus and no context. This is why context is so critically important when reading and studying the Scriptures. As we open our Bibles, we should always remember the C.I.A. method: Context + Interpretation = Application. Understanding the context will allow for more precision in your interpretation; only then will you have the key to applying it to your life. Your first step is to understand what it means to study God's Word in its proper context.

There was a time when Christians carried their Bibles to church with them. One of the most worshipful sounds I remember hearing in those days was when the pastor encouraged the congregation to turn in their Bibles to a passage of Scripture, which was followed by the rushing noise of shifting pages fluttering throughout the auditorium. I rarely hear that sound anymore. Of course, electronic Bible resources have in some sense replaced the sound of physical pages, although this has been contested recently as a greater number of adults have said they continue to use a printed version of the Bible.

Still, few would argue the fact that today only a minority of Christians are committed to bringing the Scriptures to church with them. And why would they? Will the sermon even reference the Bible? In some churches the sermon will, at best, pluck a few passages here or there and then force them together somehow. This is why context is so vitally important. We must be better Bible students by (1) reading the Bible through first-century eyes, (2) understanding the intent of the biblical authors, and (3) applying the timeless truths from each passage to our lives today.

The ideal way to study the Bible is to seek to clarify the meaning of one single passage of Scripture at a time. It usually is best not to attempt to survey a theme in one or more biblical books, but rather focus on a given passage or pericope. There are several steps that should be taken, and these steps are more easily understood when framed as questions:

1. *Summary of Passage*: What does this passage contain or say? Here the Bible student attempts to put the contents of the passage under study into their own words. At this point it might be appropriate to raise some of the important questions associated with the passage.

2. *Assessment of Immediate Context*: What paragraphs immediately precede and follow the passage? In what ways does the passage under study fit into the contextual chain?

3. *Assessment of Broad Context*: What is the thrust of the entire biblical book in which the passage occurs? Is the passage part of a larger theme or emphasis in the biblical book?

4. *Consideration of Major Problems or Questions in Passage*: What literary form is the passage, or what forms are in the passage? For example, is it

poetry, prophecy, history, a letter? Are there difficult words, phrases, allusions, or Old Testament quotations that call for further clarification? These questions are often solved through word studies and other comparative work. Are there textual problems, e.g., a verse missing in some manuscripts? Are there any unusual parallels with other writings, inside or outside the Bible? Does the passage allude to a historical event?

5. *Interpretation of Passage*: In light of the above research, what does the passage mean?

6. *Conclusion*: In light of what the passage means, how is the biblical book in which the passage is found to be understood?

Research Tools

It sometimes helps to use outside resources to guide you in your study of the Bible. These can include:

1. *Religion Index One* and *Religion Index Two* (look up Bible passages in the subject index; some of the more recent volumes also have a Scripture index).

2. Journal articles (as indicated by the above indexes).

3. Good commentaries (not surveys or devotionals, but recent commentaries).

4. Bible dictionaries, concordances, and encyclopedias.

Going Deeper

Always study a passage from one of the four Gospels by comparing it to what is said in the other Gospels. For example, if you're studying a passage from Matthew, then observe how closely Matthew has followed Mark in telling the same story. Or if you're studying a passage from Mark, observe how that passage is presented in Matthew or Luke. Be sure to ask this question: What issue(s) was the evangelist addressing?

If you're studying a passage in one of Paul's letters, be sure to consider the letter in the context of the apostle's ministry as a whole—e.g., the book of Acts. What was Paul's relationship with the particular church for whom he wrote the letter? What had Paul experienced while with them and later when he wrote his letter?

If you're studying an Old Testament passage, try to fit it into Israel's history (e.g., a passage of Isaiah and the proper place in 2 Kings). If the passage contains an allusion to or a direct quotation from the Old Testament, consider the following steps:

1. What OT version does the NT quotation represent? Does it derive from the Hebrew (i.e., the MT), from the Greek (i.e., the LXX), or from the Aramaic (i.e., the Targum)?

2. How does the NT quotation compare with the above OT versions? Are there differences, and if so, what do you make of the differences?

3. Discover what other first century (or thereabouts) literatures quote or allude to the OT text and try

to figure out what the various interpretations and applications were. These literatures would include: (a) Apocrypha; (b) Pseudepigrapha; (c) Qumran; and (d) Rabbinic (i.e., Mishnah, Tosefta, Talmud, early Midrashim, and early Targums).

Check to see if the passage contains any textual variants that call for comment. It's possible that the meaning of the passage may depend on which variant is thought to reflect the original form of the Greek text. For example, in Romans 5:1, it's either "having been justified by faith, we have [ἔχομεν] peace with God," or "having been justified by faith, let us have [ἔχωμεν] peace with God." In a few cases, an entire pericope may be in doubt (e.g., John 7:53–8:11, the woman caught in adultery; Mark 16:9–20). There are textual variants in the Hebrew literature too.

What about the Apocrypha?

Old Testaments in some churches include what we call the Apocrypha. The word *Apocrypha* means "hidden" or "doubtful." There are about 14 or 15 apocryphal books, depending on how they're counted. For centuries, Christians read the apocryphal books in addition to the 39 Old Testament books. In the sixteenth century, Martin Luther did not recognize the apocryphal books, and as a result our modern Bibles, which are based on Luther's Protestant canon, don't include the apocryphal writings. The Roman Catholic Church, however, maintained the status of the Apocrypha as holy Scripture, and at the Council of Trent in 1548, the church formally canonized them.

Up to this point, these books had been read and studied but not taken as seriously as the 39 books in the Old Testament. They were like an appendix to the library of the Old Testament. The Apocrypha helps us to understand events taking place in Israel during the period between the Old and New Testaments. These books fill in some noticeable gaps in our knowledge of the Second Temple. The books of Maccabees are especially useful in this regard. Other books, like the Wisdom of Solomon and Ecclesiasticus, help us better understand Jewish piety and the interpretation of Scripture in the generations immediately leading up to the time of Jesus.

Jerome included the apocryphal books in his Bible translation, albeit with a qualifier. He distinguished the canonical books from the ecclesiastical books or Apocrypha. Jerome described the Apocrypha as "helpful but not inspired." Therefore, it's helpful for us to know what these books contain. Just because we study books outside the 66 in the Bible doesn't mean we regard them as inspired Scripture or that they ought to be part of the Bible.

Don't Be Intimidated to Study for Yourself

The Bible can be read and studied by all and with no prerequisites. The tools I've laid out in this chapter will guide you on the road of correct biblical interpretation and application. There are many good translations of the Bible to choose from. Just remember this: People risked their lives to translate the Bible, and God preserved it through the centuries for you to read, so don't be afraid to do so. In the new world of artificial intelligence, we look to a book that is eternal. We look to God to find a moral compass, a guidebook for life. The Bible is a good book because it is God's book.

Most importantly, when you're studying God's Word, keep in mind the big picture: This book was written by God and delivered by the Holy Spirit. Its focus is Jesus and God's redemption of a broken world. This should be our focus too as we study what God has said to us, his people.

9　What Is Meditation?

Bible study should be fresh and fulfilling rather than dry and dusty, and the difference comes down to what or who we are pursuing. In Philippians 3:10, Paul said his goal was "that I may know him and the power of his resurrection." Similarly, that is the primary goal of Bible study—knowing more and more about Jesus because to know him is to love him, and to love him is to serve him.

We often call our time alone with God a quiet time. Why a quiet time? Because it's in the silence that we hear the "still small voice" of God (1 Kings 19:12 NKJV). The purpose of silence for the Christian is to listen to God's Word, because when the Bible speaks, God speaks. We must be intentional about turning off social media while seeking stillness and solitude and silence. I challenge you to try this. Open God's Word in a quiet place at a specific time. Wait on God. Read. Listen. God's Spirit will illuminate a passage and will enlighten your mind and enable you to see things clearly. God's Word will help you to think clearly, which is wisdom, and give you the ability to make good decisions. Your faith will be strengthened.

This silence and waiting on God can also be called "meditation." Meditation is the practice of deep thinking and deep focus on God and his Word. It is a spiritual exercise that many have neglected. According to author and Bible teacher Robert Morgan, meditation is not new, and it is not New Age. God, not the gurus, devised it, and it is based on the Bible, not on Buddha. Biblical meditation is an antidote to the unprecedented stress of our age. In a world where everyone is overwhelmed and undervalued, our survival, sanity, and saintliness depend on reclaiming the lost art of biblical meditation. This practice can dramatically lessen your anxiety, reduce your stress, and leave you with an ocean's depth of inner peace.

We all need a balanced spiritual diet. Just as we require nutritious food for our bodies, we need to consume God's Word in a way that fuels us properly. Here is how my friend Chuck Swindoll put it: "Our souls long to be fed, nourished, and energized by the Scriptures on a regular basis. When we fail to set aside time to digest healthy spiritual food, it isn't long before the consequences start to kick in. And it's not a pretty sight. We start to operate out of the flesh rather than the control of God's Spirit. We become shallow and selfish, more demanding and less gentle. We react impatiently, irrationally and angrily. These are telltale signs of inner malnutrition."[1]

Spiritual malnutrition is a major issue among Christians. Rather than eating and getting energy from a delicious meal in God's Word, too often we're consuming the junk food of social media, scrolling through somebody else's life and wasting hour after hour of our valuable time—time we could be spending growing in the faith and developing our spiritual muscles. Let's not be constantly entertaining ourselves with mindless activities that harm the Spirit. Ask yourself, How much time am I spending each day staring at my phone as compared to the time I spend reading and pondering Scripture? Let's resolve to be diligent in this matter, regularly turning to the Word of God, meditating on him and his message for us.

In meditating on God's Word, we must be willing to read deeply and prayerfully, applying its meaning and message to our lives. The Bible is not a book for the casual reader. Every Christian should take to heart the admonition of Paul to Timothy: "Do your best to present yourself to God as one approved, a worker who has no need to be ashamed, rightly handling the word of truth" (2 Timothy 2:15). Paul's challenge to his protégé Timothy was to work hard and to study the Scripture, so that God would approve, and the young pastor would be equipped for service and ministry.

Many Bible plans are available to select from to help you read the Bible, whether in its entirety or portions of it such as key passages. What's most important is that we read God's Word regularly and repeatedly. When you come to a passage of Scripture, read it thoughtfully and focus on what you're hearing and what God is saying. Don't rush. Resist the urge to skim through it. Pause and reread, mulling over the words. Remember, every word is God's Word.

You may want to read the Bible aloud or listen to the Bible being read to you by someone else via podcast or audiobook. This past year I was approached by friends at Pray.com about a reading-through-the-Bible project called *The Bible in a Year*. The goal was to provide an introduction and an application to each passage as we read through the Bible from Genesis to Revelation. It was a daunting but delightful task. Day by day we walked through the Scripture. Initially, I thought maybe a few thousand people would want to read the Bible by listening to God's Word in this way, but in the end over 50 million people (and growing) have downloaded the podcast and are regularly reading the Bible with us. I would encourage you to join us. But however you choose to read the Bible, start by reading it all the way through. "Practice these things, immerse yourself in them, so that all may see your progress" (1 Timothy 4:15).

What God Calls Us to Dwell On

In Philippians 4:6–9, we're told not to worry about anything, but to pray about everything. After this the text says whatever is true, honorable, just, pure, lovely, and commendable, that we should think about these things. We're called to think clearly and focus particularly on the things of God. This is what I call "biblical mindfulness." When people speak of meditation today, they're often thinking of New Age meditation or maybe Hinduism or Buddhism. But what I'm talking about here isn't any of that. I'm talking about the Bible on your brain. We must think clearly about God's Word, God's precepts, his principles and promises. Psalm 119:147 says, "I rise before dawn and cry for help; I hope in your words." Let's take the time to meditate on God's Word.

Picture a cow chewing its cud, regurgitating the food and eating it again and again. It's not a beautiful metaphor, but you get the picture. The Navigators, a biblical memory organization and discipleship group, teach Christians to memorize, visualize, and personalize the Scripture. That's a good way of looking at it—to meditate and concentrate on the truth of God's Word. It will change the way you think and live. Be open to truth and let God speak to you in the depths of your heart.

Journaling and Note-Taking

One other piece to add to the meditation process is to write down your thoughts. Keep a journal or personal notebook close by (or use a note-taking app on your phone) so you can copy Bible verses for memorization and further meditation. When we take notes, we better remember what we have read and preserve our thoughts for the future. Don't lose what God is saying to you in his Word.

Next, mark up your Bible. As I've read my Bible through the years, I've underlined verses, highlighted them, and taken notes in the margins. Some people think it's irreverent to mark up a Bible, but the way I look at it, a Bible marked up and worn belongs to someone whose life isn't. Your Bible and the notes you write within it say something about you. The verses you underscore become a kind of spiritual history of your walk with the Lord. Also, you can leave your marked-up Bible to your family as a legacy. What a lasting treasure your Bible would be to them. Therefore, I'd encourage you to mark up your Bible and make your reading and studying personal.

Pray It In

Another key part of the meditation process is to pray God's Word back to him. After you've read a passage of Scripture, pray over the words and personalize them. The psalmist said, "Open my eyes, that I may behold wondrous things out of your law" (Psalm 119:18). There are many prayers like this one in the Bible, from the prayers of the psalmist (the heart cry) to the prayers of the Old Testament personalities and prophets, along with the prayers of Paul and the apostles. These have been recorded to help us in our own conversations with God. Of course, there's the prayer that Jesus taught us, the Lord's Prayer, which is the perfect model (Matthew 6:9–13). Pray this Jesus prayer daily.

As you read the Bible, you can also turn its promises, principles, and precepts into prayers. In the book of Acts, when the early church was growing, the apostles gave themselves to prayer and the study of God's Word (Acts 6). But this is not just for the apostles; it's for all of us. One way to pray the Scripture is to take a passage and change the pronouns by making them personal. When a passage speaks to you personally, turn it into a prayer of petition, adoration, intercession, or confession. And when you come to a passage of Scripture that inspires you, thank God for his truth and ask the Holy Spirit to teach you and enable you to live out what you are learning.

Live It Out

I want to remind you that the Bible is a living book—the breath of God is in it. Every time we open the Scriptures and open our hearts, God breathes life into us. And so we must live it out. This is how we apply God's Word to our daily lives, making it personal and practical. James, the half brother of our Lord, said, "Be doers of the word, and not hearers only, deceiving yourselves" (James 1:22). He also said that faith without works is dead (James 2:17). The Bible is to be learned, but also lived in obedience to God. Proverbs 1:1–3 says, "These are the wise sayings of Solomon, David's son, Israel's king—Written down so we'll know how to live well and right, to understand what life means and where it's going; A manual for living, for learning what's right and just and fair; To teach the inexperienced the ropes and give our young people a grasp on reality" (THE MESSAGE).

When you pray with an open Bible, God's Word with all its promises will grow in your soul. You not only know how to pray but what to pray as the Word penetrates your mind and heart. Billy Graham said prayer by itself is like a diet without protein. Prayer is important to our spiritual growth, but of even greater importance is God's Word, the Bible. When we couple God's Word with prayer, there is a dual impact on our lives. We need both God's Word and prayer if we are to grow in the Lord.

Letting God's Word Change You

When reading your Bible, meditate on the question, What am I going to do about this? Then let your mind absorb

God's answer. In the mid-1980s, I was preaching God's Word at the First Baptist Church of West Palm Beach, Florida. I was speaking boldly of the evil of abortion and how sinful it is to take a life from the womb. I believe this strongly because it is consistent with a biblical worldview. As I was preaching, this question was whispered in my own heart, as the Spirit of God seemed to say to me, *What are you going to do about it?* What are you going to do about the abortion issue? Are you just going to talk about it, or are you going to act? So I responded in silent prayer, even as I was bringing God's Word that evening, "Yes, Lord, I will do what you want me to do."

From there I learned of a crisis pregnancy center in Georgia, so I went to Georgia and looked into what they were doing to save babies and to help hurting people. After I returned to West Palm Beach, we began to organize. We founded a crisis pregnancy center that the church operated for many years. When I moved to Dallas in 1989, one of the first things we did at our church was to establish a pregnancy center. That ministry has since grown through the years to three pregnancy centers, along with two mobile units with ministry to women who are facing crisis pregnancies—not only through the births of their children but beyond, continuing to minister to their families. Over the last 30 years, we have seen over 100,000 babies saved and more than 5,000 professions of faith. That all happened because we listened to God speaking through his Word and acted in faith.

Some say that they don't understand the Bible. The agnostic and author Mark Twain once said, "It's not the parts of the Bible I don't understand that bother me, it is the parts of the Bible I do understand." I think he got that right. In other words, it's usually not that complicated to understand it enough to do what it says. The problem for most people is not *wanting* to do what it says. But the more you dwell on God's Word, the more you will grow in your faith and obedience to God.

Romans 10:17 says, "So faith comes from hearing, and hearing through the word of Christ." Along with hearing God and taking him at his Word, we then must live it out and pass it on. Joshua 1:8 says, "This Book of the Law shall not depart from your mouth, but you shall meditate on it day and night, so that you may be careful to do according to all that is written in it. For then you will make your way prosperous, and then you will have good success." In this verse, we see that obedience and meditation go hand in hand.

Do not keep your faith to yourself; the Word of God and the testimony of Jesus are to be shared with the world. We're to be witnesses of God's grace and mercy, for this is the gospel. The disciples spent three power-packed years with Jesus, walking with him, listening and learning. Jesus then sent them out into the world to proclaim the gospel and make disciples of all nations (Matthew 28:19–20). In John 20:21, he said, "As the Father has sent me, even so I am sending you."

Bible knowledge is not to be turned inward. The real evidence of our Bible knowledge is how we're developing as disciples as we share the message of hope and salvation with the world. Our witness flows out of our relationship with Christ. In John 15:5, Jesus spoke about abiding in him: "I am the vine; you are the branches. Whoever abides in me and I in him, he it is that bears much fruit, for apart from me you can do nothing."

The apostles were arrested for boldly sharing their faith in Jesus Christ despite being told never to speak the name of Jesus again. They responded courageously by saying they could not help but speak those things that they had seen and heard. When you take time in God's Word to *listen* to him, to ask his Spirit to fill your life and set you on a mission for him, you cannot help but speak what you've seen and heard. T. B. Maston, the longtime professor of Christian ethics at Southwestern Baptist Theological Seminary in Fort Worth, Texas, said this: "The Christians who have turned the world upside down have been men and women with a vision in their hearts and a Bible in their hands."

Billy Graham was once asked, if he were to do things over, would he do it differently? His honest answer was, "Yes, I would study more, I would pray more, I would travel less. I would spend more time in meditation and prayer and telling the Lord I love and adore him." This is great advice from one of the greatest Christians who ever lived. We all would benefit from more study and more praying. To study God's Word is to discover the joy and fulfillment of not only knowing the Bible yourself but passing its truth on to others. Let's all go deeper in our devotion to Bible study. May God give us an insatiable hunger for his Word.

My family and I went to one of those Brazilian steak houses where you can eat all the meat you want until you pass out. We were given a small disk. On one side it was green, and the other side red. So long as you kept the green side up, the servers would keep bringing every kind of meat you can imagine. If you go home hungry, it's your own fault. When it comes to feasting on God's Word, you can never get enough. But I assure you: You'll be filled and satisfied and will keep asking for more. This means you'll keep showing up faithfully to hear your pastor explain God's Word and what it means for godly living.

It's also why you keep getting up early or staying up late to read your Bible. It's the reason you'll want to be in a small group Bible study and search the Scriptures with like-minded believers. You can never get enough of the meat and milk of the Bible. I can tell you that after all these years of seriously studying God's Word, there is still in me an insatiable appetite to learn more and more of what God says in his book. It's been said that the Bible makes bad men good, and good men better. I want to be a better man, so I keep my nose in the Bible and my knees on the floor in prayer, hungering for all that he promises us in his Word. This is the pursuit of a lifetime. I invite you to join me at the table for this filling and fulfilling meal that satisfies our deepest longing.

In the midst of our busy days, we should carve out time to be with God by setting aside our devices, holding off returning texts and calls, and sitting quietly with an open Bible and open hearts and minds to meditate on the Word of God and our great Savior's love for us. Cathe Laurie wrote, "How often do you look up to see the sky, the trees, the birds? When you do, what do you hear? I want to get out of the shallows. I want to grow deeper. It may mean I won't cover as much ground, but the treasures we're seeking are rarely found while glancing at the surface. Go deep. Slow down, focus, and worship the Lord and listen to God speak to you in his Word. Tell him you love him and that you will obey him in all things. Align your will to do the will of God. Ask him to fill you with his Spirit."[2]

It has been my consistent time spent with God that has made all the difference in my spiritual and emotional health. One of the challenges I've faced as a Christian through the years is the fear that something bad might happen. This is no doubt rooted in the early, tragic death of my father, who was brutally murdered. My mother died just a few years after that, passing away with a broken heart at the loss of her husband. At that point I began to wonder what was next. Both died on the same date in late August, five years apart. As August rolled around each year, I began to assume August was going to be a bad month. I knew that God wanted me to expect the best in life, not the worst, yet I struggled every summer with these doubts and fears. I'm an optimist by nature, and yet there was this fear in me that something horrible would happen. I was living without the constant expectation and hope that we have in God's Word.

Proverbs 13:12 says, "Hope deferred makes the heart sick." When we have hope, we believe our future is in God's hands and that we can trust him completely. Hope is one of the most powerful encouragers in our lives. We can hope and expect and believe that God will not do the worst but the best for us because God is good. Over the years, dwelling on his Word, I've learned to expect the best from God because I know God is good. I believe something good is going to happen every day. And I can truly get up each morning and say it is going to be a great day because

I've seen the favor and faithfulness of God in my life, and I believe my future is in his hands.

Hope will rise within you too as you read and meditate on the Scriptures and the promises of God. You'll soon begin to believe that something good is going to happen. Isaiah 61:7 tells us, "Instead of your shame there shall be a double portion; instead of dishonor they shall rejoice in their lot; therefore in their land they shall possess a double portion; they shall have everlasting joy." This is such a powerful Scripture because it reminds us that God blesses us over and over again. Not just one, not just two, but multiple blessings. We can embrace every day with this life-changing promise, which means that God is going to reward you.

The Amplified Bible translates the idea of a double portion by using the phrase "twofold recompense." *Recompense* isn't a word we use much today, but it simply means "reward." God is saying, *I'm going to fill you with hope and reward you, paying you back for everything you've gone through. I'm going to multiply my blessings to you.* It was a terrible thing to lose my father and go through some of the other very difficult experiences in my life, but God has more than paid me back, more than made up for every damaging thing. He has blessed me and our family beyond what we could have possibly imagined (see Ephesians 3:20). Always keep God's promises in the forefront of your mind as you feed on his Word.

Enjoying God's Word

Psalm 1 tells us that God's Word is to be enjoyed, not endured. Every word of Scripture provides a pathway to

God, which is the way to genuine happiness. The message of the Bible through and through is good news. Good news of great joy. When it comes to the Scripture, the psalmist has said that when he reads it, there is rejoicing in his soul: "In your presence there is fullness of joy; at your right hand are pleasures forevermore" (Psalm 16:11).

God wants us to enjoy life by experiencing him. The Westminster Confession of Faith puts it this way: "The chief end of man is to glorify God and enjoy him forever." When we read and reflect on God's Word, we begin to know him more and therefore love him more. To know him is to love him, and to love him is to enjoy his presence.

What does it take to make us happy? Harvard professor Arthur C. Brooks, who specializes in happiness studies, gives his perspective in an interview with *Harvard Business Review*. Happiness started to devolve into a state of malaise beginning in the late 1980s and early '90s, declining a bit more with each passing year during this period. Then it took a significant dip when social media came along. Social media, says Brooks, was catastrophic for happiness. There's a lot of neuroscience behind this, yet everybody knows that when people feel bored or lonely, they turn to their devices. However, this actually makes them more bored and even lonelier. It's a huge problem, especially for young adults.

Then the coronavirus came along, which was the most catastrophic event for public happiness worldwide that we've seen in a long time. Ordinarily, about 30 percent of people would say they're very happy with their lives, and 15 percent would say they're not happy. The rest land somewhere in the middle. Those numbers are now flipped: 30 percent are not happy, and 15 percent are very happy.[3]

What's the answer to increasing our happiness? According to Brooks, it has everything to do with our social lives and with our love relationships. It's your family life, your real relationships, and work that serves other people. These have been in decline, and there is no technology that's going to solve the problem.

Brooks's findings are true, but they don't go quite far enough. Yes, happiness is about relationships, but he missed out on the most important relationship of all: our relationship with God. As you read the Bible, you'll discover that ultimate, lasting happiness is found in knowing God and both experiencing and expressing his love. The Bible has been called God's love letter. To understand Scripture, it is essential to be a follower of Jesus, his disciple. When we know the Lord, we are included in his family, and God has written and shared the family secrets with all of us—secrets we should share with others.

The Word of God is for the child of God, and it is understood because of the Spirit of God (see 1 Corinthians 2:10–16). To comprehend the Bible, you must have a relationship with God through Jesus Christ. The purpose of the Scripture is to introduce and invite us into a loving devotion to God, and the key to interpreting the Scripture is knowing Christ, walking in the Spirit, and living according to his Word. The Bible is Christocentric—Jesus Christ is the center. He is the core and circumference of the Bible. He is the source and the subject and the story of the Bible (see Colossians 1:15–20). I cannot stress this enough. It is Jesus and he alone who makes the Bible a living thing, for he is Life.

When we have a relationship with Christ, we are then blessed and have received every blessing from him. The word *blessed* can also be translated as *happy*. Happy is the one whose life is planted deep in God's Word. The believer's life is blessed when it's built upon the words of the Bible. This life is full, complete, satisfying, and strong. True happiness is not about how we feel, for it's possible to feel unhappy and happy at the same time. Positive and negative emotions may coexist. Yet in Christ, always within us there resides a blessedness, an abiding joy. We are planted like solid trees near the water, delighting in the Word of God that he's given to us: "But his delight is in the law of the LORD, and on his law he meditates day and night" (Psalm 1:2). We can live rejoicing because when storms come, and they always do, we remain firm in our faith, a faith that is deeply rooted in the truth of God's Word.

In Matthew 7, Jesus spoke of two men who built houses, one on the rock and the other on the sand: "Everyone then who hears these words of mine and does them will be like a wise man who built his house on the rock. And the rain fell, and the floods came, and the winds blew and beat on that house, but it did not fall, because it had been founded on the rock. And everyone who hears these words of mine and does not do them will be like a foolish man who built his house on the sand. And the rain fell, and the floods came, and the winds blew and beat against that house, and it fell, and great was the fall of it" (Matthew 7:24–27).

Notice the man who built his life on the rock. The rock is Jesus, the Rock of Ages, and this man survived the storm—unlike the foolish man who built on sand. Building our lives on Jesus through the knowledge and wisdom of his Word is the greatest source of happiness and blessing we could ever hope for.

10 The Bible and Spiritual Warfare

There is a backstory to the Bible. Behind the scenes of Scripture, a cosmic battle is being waged between God and Satan, between good and evil, light and darkness, the kingdom of God and the kingdoms of this world. This battle began sometime in ages past when an angelic being called Lucifer rose up in rebellion against God. Before there was rebellion on earth and sin in the Garden of Eden, there was revolt in heaven. Isaiah gives us a glimpse of what happened before time as we know it began. Lucifer, the beautiful angel of light, became the angel and prince of darkness and was removed from the heavenly hosts, along with one third of the angelic beings, who joined him in this rebellion. This is when the war of the ages was launched (Isaiah 14:12–14).

And this is how the devil became the devil, a powerful spiritual opponent to God and his kingdom. The devil is often characterized as a cartoonish character dressed in a red suit with horns, carrying a pitchfork and living in hell. He's viewed by many as just a myth or as a misunderstood medieval figure who doesn't literally exist. You may have been told that Satan is only a symbol of evil, but the Bible—our only authoritative source of truth on the subject—tells us the devil is a real being, the enemy and the adversary of followers of Christ. The devil "prowls around like a roaring lion, seeking someone to devour" (1 Peter 5:8). He comes to kill, steal, and destroy, and his name means slanderer or accuser. Stu Weber says, "Know it or not, like it or not, you and I are in a war, and we need to begin living as if we were in a battle for our lives because in fact we are.[1]

The New Testament is filled with Scriptures that warn us of this war, not to scare us but to prepare us to fight spiritual battles. The most well-known of these passages is Ephesians 6:10–12: "Finally, be strong in the Lord and in the strength of his might. Put on the whole armor of God, that you may be able to stand against the schemes of the devil. For we do not wrestle against flesh and blood, but against the rulers, against the authorities, against the cosmic powers over this present darkness, against the spiritual forces of evil in the heavenly places."

We Christians are commanded to be soldiers in God's army, strong and courageous and victorious in spiritual battle. Our strength for the battle is not our own, but God's mighty power at work in us. We've been given spiritual weapons for spiritual warfare and are equipped to win. We're to put on the whole armor of God and take up the sword of the Spirit, which is the Word of God (Ephesians 6:17). The word Paul uses to describe this sword is *machaira*, which is a short, dagger-like blade made for hand-to-hand combat. It is sharp and is deadly in that it pierces the heart. Again, I reiterate Hebrews 4:12, which says, "For the word of God is living and active, sharper than any two-edged sword, piercing to the division of soul and of spirit, of joints and of marrow, and discerning the thoughts and intentions of the heart." Satan and his demonic minions are no match for the Word of God, and they are run through by the sword of the Spirit.

Jesus proved this in the wilderness when Satan tempted him, and he used God's Word to ward off the attacks. When trials and temptations come, when Satan attacks you, be ready to defeat him with Scripture, the sword of the Spirit. Satan is overcome when we, like Jesus, use God's Word against him. "Resist the devil, and he will flee from you" (James 4:7).

Once you read the Bible through, you'll notice that it is a book filled with battles throughout the history of Israel. God's chosen people are commanded to take those territories rightfully belonging to them, and even to this day, the Jewish people continue to fight for their survival. In these battles of the Old Testament, God often raised up champions and spiritual heroes who, according to Paul, would be examples to us. In Hebrews 11, we meet the heroes who inspire and motivate us as Bible-believing Christians. Consequently, we love God's people of Israel and prayerfully support their right to exist and to flourish in the land God has given them. Through the Jewish people, God gave us the Bible and our Messiah, the Lord Jesus. This is a thread that runs throughout the Scriptures.

Satan's Tactics

The word *Satan* means "adversary" or "oppressor." Satan hates and attacks everything and everyone God loves. He is deceptive and dangerous, and he means to destroy you, your family, your faith, and your friends. He inflicts pain and suffering and unleashes hate and hell upon the world. He uses doubt, disappointment, and deceit, and he "disguises himself as an angel of light" (2 Corinthians 11:14). As Christians, we must take this ruthless enemy and our spiritual warfare seriously. Unfortunately, too many don't seem to realize that we're living in a war zone, and they risk becoming casualties due to their ignorance.

When we live according to God's Word, we become better equipped for spiritual battle, just as Paul tells us in Ephesians 6. Never forget that the Bible is both trustworthy and authoritative. As you wield the sword of the Spirit (the Bible) in spiritual warfare, you can be sure that "no weapon that is fashioned against you shall succeed" (Isaiah 54:17). You have the mighty power of God's Word at your disposal. For the weapons of our warfare are not human (2 Corinthians 10:4); the Word of God in connection with the Spirit of God is your superpower.

When I preach God's Word, it is with the power of the Holy Spirit. I'm engaging in spiritual battle and taking souls from enemy territory. What is true for me is true for you. When you share your faith in Jesus, when you share the gospel of Christ, you're in a spiritual battle and are defeating the enemy. Revelation 12:11 says, "They have conquered him by the blood of the Lamb and by the word of their testimony. . . ." Our testimony is the Word of God and the power of his blood to save us, which is the message of the Bible. I've seen God's Word save the lost, comfort the saved, penetrate the darkness of the devil's domain, and destroy the strongholds of addiction, setting captives free. Jesus said, "You will know the truth, and the truth will set you free" (John 8:32). So put on the armor of God, sharpen your sword, and get in the battle, knowing that "he who is in you is greater than he who is in the world" (1 John 4:4).

The battlefield for warfare is prayer, so take up "the sword of the Spirit, which is the word of God, praying at all times in the Spirit . . ." (Ephesians 6:17–18). There's an inseparable connection between prayer and God's Word, which we can see in Acts 6:4 as the leaders of the early church gave themselves to the Word of God and to prayer. Jesus promised, "If you abide in me, and my words abide in you, ask whatever you wish, and it will be done for you" (John 15:7). When we pray according to God's Word, we are praying in alignment with God's will; our prayers will be informed and inspired by the Bible. The power of his Word, together with its principles and promises, guarantees our spiritual victory.

Victory in Christ

Whatever comes against us from the world, the flesh, and the devil is no match for the Word of God and the testimony of Jesus. When you know the Bible, you'll be certain of the outcome of this war that has been raging for so long. God has promised us victory and has already given it to us. I have a T-shirt that says *Jesus Won* across its front—not "Jesus Wins" or "He will win." Jesus already won, as the enemy, Satan, was defeated at the cross. In Christ we have victory over Satan, sin, death, and hell. The victory that Christ has won is now ours.

I read an interview in the *Wall Street Journal* that featured the famous novelist John Grisham. It described his habits and personal disciplines of writing, which allow him to produce at least one book per year. I was interested to discover that he writes the last chapter of his stories first. Similarly, we have read the last chapters of God's Word, so we know how this story ends. When Jesus died on the cross, he exclaimed, "It is finished." *Tetelestai*. This doesn't mean, however, that he was finished—he was far from finished. No, Satan was finished, and the work of salvation was accomplished at the cross.

When you know the victory is complete, you can begin living with a new perspective. You can anticipate the day when you will lay down your sword because the battle is over, and you'll celebrate for all of eternity. Your victory is in Jesus. No wonder the apostle Paul, though facing execution, was able to say he had a desire to depart and to be with Christ, which was far better: "For to me to live is Christ, and to die is gain" (Philippians 1:21).

CONCLUSION

Surrendering Your Life to Jesus Christ

The Jesus book is the story of salvation, and a scarlet thread of redemption runs through its pages from beginning to end. It is the one book that tells us how to go to heaven and spend eternity with the Lord. In a world of confusion, chaos, and uncertainty, the only thing that is steady and sure is the God who holds our future in the palm of his hand. When we endeavor to know this good and gracious God, we find we also come to know perfect peace. Peace regarding our identity, peace regarding our circumstances, and peace regarding our destination following death. Relating intimately with God is essential to our well-being, both now and forever.

Therefore, it's important that I clearly share God's one and only way to eternal life. Jesus said, "I am the way, and the truth, and the life. No one comes to the Father except through me" (John 14:6). The Bible says that God has put eternity in our hearts and that we can know beyond the shadow of a doubt that we will spend eternity with him—relating with him, worshiping him, and exploring the mysteries that have always racked our brains (Ecclesiastes 3:11). And the way we arrive at this certainty is by simply believing in Christ. Finally, 1 John 5:13 says, "I write these things to you who believe in the name of the Son of God that you may know that you have eternal life."

This is the essence of grace, that because of Jesus Christ's intervention in our lives, we can forever be present with God.

Grasping God's Grace

The word *grace* simply means "gift," and that's exactly what our salvation is: It is a free gift from God that we can't earn or deserve. We can do nothing more than receive it. "For by grace you have been saved through faith," says Ephesians 2:8–9. "And this is not your own doing; it is the gift of God, not a result of works, so that no one may boast." It is not our good deeds that make us Christians; it's our acceptance of God's gift of grace.

Grace was necessary for the following four reasons:

1. *Everyone has sinned.*

    The Bible is clear that "all have sinned and fall short of the glory of God" (Romans 3:23). This means that every person has broken God's commandments and missed the mark as it relates to his standard of righteousness. We can be "good" in the eyes of others, but in our hearts we know something is amiss. We acknowledge that we often fail to do the things we want to do and instead do the very things we shouldn't do. When it comes to Jesus' command for us to "be perfect, as your heavenly Father is perfect" (Matthew 5:48), we know our track record leaves much to be desired.

2. *Our sin deserves punishment.*

Romans 6:23 explains that our sin deserves not a breezy warning or a few community-service hours; our sin is deserving of death. So even as our heavenly Father deeply loves us, he can't overlook our sin. Habakkuk 1:13 says that God has "purer eyes than to see evil and cannot look at wrong." His holiness demands payment for our terrible sin; in his view, justice must be served. There is a saying in our courts of law that if a judge knowingly releases a guilty man, the judge himself is condemned. God, the Judge of the earth, cannot turn a blind eye to our sin because in doing so, he'd be breaking his own law. This would make Almighty God a sinner, something his character absolutely won't allow. Herein lies the dilemma: How is God supposed to love us while at the same time judge our sin?

3. *Jesus paid the price for our sin.*

God's solution to the grand dilemma we faced was to ask his Son to pay the penalty for our sin. And fortunately, Jesus complied. The Bible declares, "In the beginning was the Word, and the Word was with God, and the Word was God . . . And the Word became flesh and dwelt among us . . ." (John 1:1, 14).

Jesus Christ is God in the flesh. He is just as much God as if he were not man, and just as much man as if he were not God. And at a specific point in history, he came from heaven to earth to reveal the love of God for us.

Jesus Christ made it possible for us to go to heaven by dying on the cross. In that great act of love, he paid the price for our sins and purchased a place in heaven for us that he now offers as a free gift. He took our place of judgment, and the wrath of God that burns against sin fell solely and completely on his Son: "For our sake he made him to be sin who knew no sin, so that in him we might become the righteousness of God" (2 Corinthians 5:21).

So while we cannot earn, learn, or deserve salvation, we can receive it because of Jesus' work and sacrifice on the cross. And the way we receive salvation is by faith.

4. *Forgiveness can be ours.*

Some people possess an "intellectual" faith—that is, a faith in the facts of the gospel or in the historical record concerning Jesus Christ. In one sense, this type of faith is akin to belief in George Washington, Abraham Lincoln, or any other notable historical figure. They believe these people existed, but that belief doesn't affect their lives. There are others who possess "circumstantial" faith, which compels them to look to God during a crisis or unsettling event, but then their faith falls flat once the circumstances abate.

The Bible talks about a third type of faith, the only saving faith that exists. It says that true faith in Jesus Christ involves choosing to turn from sin and to live fully dependent on him. This saving faith comes by simple belief: "Believe in the Lord Jesus, and you will be saved" (Acts 16:31). This is how we come to know God and receive forgiveness for our sins.

Responding by Faith

If you have never trusted Jesus Christ alone for your salvation, you can do so today. Tell God that you are ready to surrender to him your entire life—your thoughts, your words, your attitudes, your actions—knowing that as soon as you open the door to your heart, according to Revelation 3:20, he will readily and gladly come in: "Behold, I stand at the door and knock. If anyone hears my voice and opens the door, I will come in to him."

Pray a simple prayer, such as the one that follows:

Heavenly Father, I am a sinner in need of your gift of grace. I turn from trusting in myself and my good works to trusting in you alone to be saved. I know that your Son, Jesus, died on the cross for my sins, that he was buried and rose again that I might have life everlasting. Come into my life, Father, by your Holy Spirit. I invite you to take control of my life and make me the person you want me to be. Thank you for seeing me, for knowing me, for loving me, and for saving me now. It is in the powerful, unparalleled name of Jesus that I pray. Amen.

If you prayed the prayer above—and meant it—then
you have already begun walking in new life. The Bible has
wonderful things to say about those who submit themselves to the lordship of Jesus Christ. Let these marvelous
words soak deep into your spirit as you read:

- "I write these things to you who believe in the
  name of the Son of God that you may know that
  you have eternal life" (1 John 5:13).
- "Now to him who is able to keep you from stum-
  bling and to present you blameless before the presence of his glory with great joy, to the only God,
  our Savior, through Jesus Christ our Lord, be glory,
  majesty, dominion, and authority, before all time
  and now and forever. Amen" (Jude 24–25).
- "Consequently, he is able to save to the uttermost
  those who draw near to God through him, since he
  always lives to make intercession for them" (Hebrews 7:25).
- "And I am sure of this, that he who began a good
  work in you will bring it to completion at the day
  of Jesus Christ" (Philippians 1:6).
- "Truly, truly, I say to you, whoever hears my word
  and believes him who sent me has eternal life. He
  does not come into judgment, but has passed from
  death to life" (John 5:24).
- "I give them eternal life, and they will never perish, and no one will snatch them out of my hand"
  (John 10:28).

- "No, in all these things we are more than con-
  querors through him who loved us. For I am sure
  that neither death nor life, nor angels nor rulers,
  nor things present nor things to come, nor powers, nor height nor depth, nor anything else in
  all creation, will be able to separate us from the
  love of God in Christ Jesus our Lord" (Romans
  8:37–39).

- "In him you also, when you heard the word of
  truth, the gospel of your salvation, and believed in
  him, were sealed with the promised Holy Spirit,
  who is the guarantee of our inheritance until we
  acquire possession of it, to the praise of his glory"
  (Ephesians 1:13–14).

Knowing Jesus Christ as Savior is the most fulfilling experience this life can afford. Enjoy the journey as you allow
the Holy Spirit to shape you and transform you, guide you
and instruct you in the ways of this amazing faith.

Once we become believers, it's important that we grow
in our faith, with a commitment to worship and the ministry of a local church, that we pray consistently, and as
we've established throughout this book, that we read and
study God's Word daily. Add to that your personal witness in Christ, and you have the recipe for a maturing,
dynamic, Spirit-filled life as a believer, faithfully serving
and loving the Lord Jesus. There will be many tests, trials, and temptations that come your way, and we must all
lean hard into the race before us, trusting God and taking
him at his Word.

Final Thoughts on God's Word and the Testimony of Christ

There is no substitute for God's Word in your life. Whether you are a new Christian or a veteran believer, we all desperately need the Word of God, and we never grow beyond that need. Could it be that you have neglected God's Word and find yourself spiritually dry, in need of renewal and personal revival? Many churches need a revival of the Bible. These churches are abandoning God's Word and a biblical worldview. As a result, their congregations have become listless and passive, and they've gotten off track in the call to proclaim Christ and teach the Bible.

Frankly, preaching Christ requires the preaching of his Word. I hear a lot of good ministers today preaching good sermons, oratorical gems, but without the Word of God and the testimony of Jesus. Several years ago, after our church's Christmas production, one of our pastors was talking to someone who had attended. When asked how he liked the production, the man answered, "It wasn't my thing." When the pastor asked why, the man said, "Too much Jesus." I can't think of a better compliment for our church and its ministry.

I don't know about you, but I can't get enough of Jesus. So often churches have become lifeless and therefore powerless. There's hardly any Scripture and barely a mention of Jesus. Scripture and Christ go hand in hand. In the sermons and in worship, congregations are revived when the Scripture takes its proper place of authority in the church. In Nehemiah 8, after the godly layman Nehemiah led the children of Israel in the rebuilding of the walls around Jerusalem, there was an outcry for the Word of God. The people cried, "Bring us the book." They were assembled in the square before the Water Gate, where the Word of God was opened, and revival came to the people. It was a powerful display of what can happen in a person's life and in the life of the Church.

We echo this call to "bring us the book" because there's a famine in the land of "hearing the words of the Lord" (Amos 8:11). May our churches and pastors and teachers and institutions believe God's Word as never before. Let us trust his Word and take him at his Word. In the end, we believe the Bible because it is the Jesus book, inspired by the Holy Spirit.

I began with the story of Jesus on the road to Emmaus with two discouraged disciples. On this seven-mile trek, a miracle took place as Jesus shared Scripture. The two disciples' hearts burned with renewed faith and devotion to the risen Lord. This same Jesus walks with us today. He opens the Scriptures and by his Spirit reveals himself every step of the way. He is "the same yesterday and today and forever" (Hebrews 13:8), and so is his Word in our ever-changing, chaotic world. His Word is immutable and unchanging. Believe the Bible because it is *his* Bible. It is the Jesus book.

I pray you are convinced the Bible is God's truth through and through and that it's real and relevant and trustworthy. A true and trustworthy companion for your life. This is the reason we read it and apply its truths. Jesus, the Living Word of God, steps from the pages of his book and right into our souls.

The goal of this book about the Book of books is that you would come to love God's Word and the Savior whose story it tells. This is not a textbook, but rather a message from the heart of a pastor who has trusted God's Word, studied it, preached it, prayed it, and sought to obey it over a lifetime. You can live and die believing God's Word more and more. Let's commit to knowing and understanding the Bible better. And as we do, we will come face-to-face with the Savior who gave us his living Word.

NOTES

Chapter 1: Why You Can Trust the Bible

1. "Simple Steps to Solid Study," Grace to You website, https://www.gty.org/library/articles/A258/simple-steps-to-solid-study, accessed January 26, 2024.

2. Ken Hemphill, *Life Answers: Making Sense of Your World* (Nashville: LifeWay, 1993), 39.

Chapter 2: The Big Picture of the Bible

1. Josh McDowell and Sean McDowell, *Evidence That Demands a Verdict: Life-Changing Truth for a Skeptical World* (Nashville: Thomas Nelson Publishers, 2017).

Chapter 4: Reading the Bible as a Lens to See the World

1. See "U.S. Suicides Reached a Record High Last Year. Older men are at highest risk, while suicide rates among young people have declined," in https://www.wsj.com/health/healthcare/americans-suicide-highest-level-2022-02eb10ea?reflink=integratedwebview_share, accessed November 29, 2023.

2. Professor Arthur Holmes was not the only Christian intellectual who said important things about the mind, about worldview, and about the Christian academy. Holmes was anticipated by Harry Blamires, whose book *The Christian Mind: How Should a Christian Think?* (1963, rev. ed. 1978) charted a course that Holmes and others

would later follow. James Sire, longtime editor at InterVarsity Press, published a book titled *Discipleship of the Mind: Learning to Love God in the Ways We Think* (1990). In 2004, Jim published a sequel aptly titled *Naming the Elephant: Worldview as a Concept* (2004). Rick Ostrander, Vice President for Academic Affairs and Professional Programs at Council for Christian Colleges and Universities, published *Why College Matters to God: Faithful Learning and Christian Higher Education* (2009). Dr. Ostrander visited HBU last year and shared his insights with our faculty and deans. My HBU colleague Nancy Pearcey, who teaches in our apologetics program, published *Total Truth: Liberating Christianity from Its Cultural Captivity* (2004). A man I greatly admire is David Dockery. Dr. Dockery served for many years and very successfully as president at Union University. He now serves as president at Southwestern Seminary. With his former colleague Gregory Hornbury, in 2002 he published *Shaping a Christian Worldview: The Foundations of Christian Higher Education*, and then in 2007, Dr. Dockery published *Renewing Minds: Serving Church and Society through Christian Higher Education* (2007). I should also mention Harry Lee Poe's *Christianity in the Academy: Teaching at the Intersection of Faith and Learning*, as well as Chris Anderson's *Teaching as Believing: Faith in the University*. Both books appeared in 2004, and both have important things to say about faith in the context of the academic enterprise. Donald Opitz and Derek Melleby's *The Outrageous Idea of Academic Faithfulness: A Guide to Students* (2007) shifts the focus away from faculty and speaks directly to students. Benjamin Wiker and Jonathan Witt's *A Meaningful World: How the Arts and Sciences Reveal the Genius of Nature* (2006) explores how the curriculum itself, including science, reveals the real meaning and value of our world.

3. Jeremiah J. Johnston, *Unimaginable: What Our World Would Be Like Without Christianity* (Bloomington, MN: Bethany House Publishers, 2017).

4. Richard Dawkins, *The Blind Watchmaker: Why the Evidence of Evolution Reveals a Universe Without Design* (New York: W. W. Norton & Company, 1986), 133.

Chapter 6: Reading the Bible Daily

1. Arnold Cole and Pamela Caudill Ovwigho, "Center for Bible Engagement," https://bttbfiles.com/web/docs/cbe/Scientific_Evidence _for_the_Power_of_4.pdf, accessed January 29, 2024.

Chapter 9: What Is Meditation?

1. Charles R. Swindoll, *Searching the Scriptures: Find the Nourishment Your Soul Needs* (Carol Stream, IL: Tyndale House Publishers, 2016), 24.

2. Cathe Laurie (@cathelaurie), Instagram post, 2023. Cathe is the founder and director of Virtue, the women's ministry at Harvest Christian Fellowship.

3. Jim Dennison, https://www.denisonforum.org/daily-article /arthur-c-brooks-secret-to-happiness/, accessed January 29, 2024.

Chapter 10: The Bible and Spiritual Warfare

1. Stu Weber, *Spirit Warriors: Strategies for the Battles Christian Men and Women Face Every Day* (Sisters, OR: Multnomah Publishers, 2003), 10.

ACKNOWLEDGMENTS

Ninette Hutchinson, my assistant, who serves our church with boundless energy, typed the original manuscript. Thank you, Ninette, for your huge contribution to this book.

Dr. Jeremiah Johnston was my wingman on this project and a constant encouragement and valued contributor. Couldn't have done it without you, Jeremiah.

Andy McGuire and the team at Bethany House, thank you for believing in the book and inspiring my writing.

The Prestonwood staff is beyond amazing. I am so very thankful for the privilege of shepherding our ministry together and for the constant support of the very best people I know.

My wife, Deb Graham, and our family make it all worthwhile. There is no greater joy than knowing that our family is built on the truth of the Jesus book.

Most of all, all praise goes to Jesus, who stepped out of His Book and into my life when I was a small boy. This journey with Jesus is my life, my joy, and my hope, now and forever.

DR. JACK GRAHAM

Author Executive Summary

Dr. Jack Graham serves as Senior Pastor of Prestonwood Baptist Church, one of the nation's largest, most dynamic congregations.

When Dr. Graham came to Prestonwood in 1989, the 8,000-member congregation responded enthusiastically to his straightforward message and powerful preaching style.

Now thriving with more than 56,000 members, Prestonwood continues to grow, reaching throughout the North Texas region. In 2006, the church launched a second location, the North Campus, in a burgeoning area

20 miles north of the Plano campus. Prestonwood also has a flourishing Spanish-language ministry, Prestonwood en Español, which includes members from more than 20 nations. And Prestonwood.Live, the online community, draws worshipers from all over the world.

Dr. Graham is a noted author of numerous books, including the latest, *Reignite: Fresh Focus for an Enduring Faith*. In this deeply personal book, Dr. Graham shares lessons he learned in the midst of crisis, offering insights on how to focus on Jesus even in the darkest of days.

His other books include: *A Man of God: Essential Priorities for Every Man's Life*; *Unseen: Angels, Satan, Heaven, Hell, and Winning the Battle for Eternity*; *Angels: Who They Are, What They Do, and Why It Matters*; *Powering Up: The Fulfillment and Fruit of a God-Fueled Life*; and *Courageous Parenting*, cowritten with his wife, Deb.

Dr. Graham's passionate biblical teaching is also seen and heard across the country and throughout the world on *PowerPoint Ministries*. Through broadcasts, online sermons, and e-mail messages, he addresses relevant, everyday issues that are prevalent in the culture and strike a chord with audiences worldwide.

In October 2022, the *Bible in a Year with Jack Graham* podcast was launched in partnership with iHeartPodcasts and Pray.com, with a cinematic feel that brings the Bible to life. Within the first week of its release, the podcast reached the top spot on the Spotify religion list, and it has now surpassed 16 million downloads.

Dr. Graham has served as Honorary Chairman of the National Day of Prayer and has helped lead various national prayer initiatives. He served as President of the Southern Baptist Convention, the largest Protestant denomination in the country with more than 14 million members. He and Deb have three children—all of them grown now and married—and eight grandchildren.

PRESENCE

Dr. Graham's influence extends beyond the walls of Prestonwood through various media platforms across North America and throughout the world:

Bible in a Year Podcast	16 million downloads
X: @JackNGraham	50,900 followers
Instagram: @JackNGraham	13,600 followers
Public Facebook Page: @ PPTMinistries	535K Likes, 620K followers
Email List of Pastors/ Influencers	3,000
Prestonwood Email List	126,044 (as of April 2023)
Prestonwood Text Database	63,736 (as of April 2023)
PowerPoint Email List	80,000 (as of April 2023)
PowerPoint YouTube Subscribers	15,600
Prestonwood YouTube Subscribers	31,900

Dr. Jack Graham and *PowerPoint Ministries* airs in 7 of the top 10 markets domestically and in over 800 markets total. Dr. Graham's sermons are broadcast in 112 countries and translated into 4 different languages. His program can be viewed in TV markets with an audience of more than 500,000 households every Sunday—with TBN, Daystar, and other local markets throughout the U.S.